Sunset

CONTAINER GARDENING

BY CYNTHIA BIX AND THE EDITORS OF SUNSET BOOKS

SUNSET PUBLISHING CORPORATION · MENLO PARK, CALIFORNIA

GARDENS FOR EVERYONE

Plants in containers are one kind of garden that anyone, anywhere, can grow. One person's garden may be as simple as a single red geranium on a city windowsill. Another's may be as ambitious as a bank of trees, shrubs, and flowers—all in pots—that transforms a patio. One person loves experimenting with new combinations of flowers in big, showy pots, while another finds satisfaction in a modest display of spring bulbs or summer annuals.

If you're a beginner, growing plants in pots is the perfect way to take the plunge into gardening. You can start small, even with a single pot and plant; containers make it easy to move on to more ambitious projects at your own pace as you gain confidence and knowledge. For the experienced gardener, growing plants in containers offers the joy of unlimited possibilities for experimenting with combinations of plants and pots.

Although arrangements created by professional gardeners may look complex, the principles behind them are really very straightforward: good plant and container choices, along with proper care. In this book, you'll find practical advice about every aspect of the process, from selecting pots to picking out plants to providing the right soil for them. And you'll find blueprints for successful container designs, along with tips for coming up with your own arrangements. Turn the pages for information and inspiration, then get ready to create your own beautiful container garden—in a single pot, or in a whole array of them.

In putting together the information in this book, we were grateful to be able to call on the expertise of many individuals. We especially thank garden writer John R. Dunmire; Michael Hibbard of Bachman's Nursery in Minneapolis, Minnesota; Sunset test garden coordinator Bud Stuckey; garden writer Susan Lang; and building writer Scott Atkinson.

For generously providing props for photos, we thank Kecia A. Baker of GardenHome in Berkeley, California.

SUNSET BOOKS

Vice-President, General Manager: Richard A. Smeby
Vice-President, Editorial Director: Bob Doyle
Production Director: Lory Day
Art Director: Vasken Guiragossian

Staff for this book:

Managing Editor and Copy Editor: Phyllis Elving
Sunset Books Senior Editor, Gardening: Suzanne Normand Eyre
Additional Text: Patricia Parrott West
Editorial Consultants: Kathleen Norris Brenzel and Philip Edinger
Photo Researcher: Tishana Peebles
Production Coordinator: Patricia S. Williams
Proofreader: Marianne Lipanovich

Art Director: Alice Rogers
Page Layouts: Phippen Design Group
Computer Production: Linda Bouchard and Joan Olson
Principal Illustrator: Mimi Osborne
Additional Illustrations: Lucy I. Sargeant, Wendy Smith-Griswold

Cover: Begonias, maidenhair fern, and vinca in an Italian terra-cotta pot. Photography by Norman A. Plate. Design by Jean Manocchio. Border photograph *(Dryopteris arguta)* by Marion Brenner.

Please visit our website at www.sunsetbooks.com

PHOTOGRAPHERS:

Scott Atkinson: 57 top, 101 bottom; **Paul M. Bowers:** 80, back cover bottom; **Ed Carey:** 20 bottom; **Glenn Christiansen:** 81 all, 90 bottom, 91 top, 103; **Peter Christiansen:** 1, 7 bottom right, 14 bottom right, 28 bottom right, 42, 43 top right, 49 top left, 55 top, 105; **Rosalind Creasy:** 7 bottom left, 56 top; **Stephen Cridland:** 29 bottom right; **Alan and Linda Detrick:** 38; **Ken Druse:** 9 top right & bottom left, 11 bottom left & right, 32–33, 44 bottom, 55 bottom, 73 top right, 84 top, 85 bottom, 102 bottom; **Derek Fell:** 43 top left; **David Goldberg:** 11 top left, 12 right, 21 right; **Lynne Harrison:** 8, 29 bottom left, 65, 70, 85 top; **Philip Harvey:** 30, 64 bottom left (both) & top; **Philip Harvey for Smith & Hawken:** 59 bottom left; **Saxon Holt:** 7 top left, 9 bottom right, 20 top, 22 bottom, 23, 28 top & bottom left, 31 top, 35, 52 left, 57 bottom, 71, 77, 78 bottom, 109 top; **John Humble:** 14 left; **Michael Landis:** 54 bottom left; **Charles Mann:** 4–5, 6 top, 7 top right, 9 top left, 10, 13 bottom right, 29 top, 39 top right, 63 top, 73 bottom left, 88, back cover top; **Terrence McCarthy:** 93 top; **Don Normark:** 15 top; **Jerry Pavia:** 13 bottom left & center, 22 top, 58, 60–61, 63 bottom, 72 bottom, 73 bottom right, 87; **Norman A. Plate:** 6 bottom, 13 top right, 19, 21 left, 24 left & right, 25 all, 26 all, 27, 31 bottom, 34, 36 top and bottom, 37 top & bottom, 39 bottom, 43 bottom, 44 top, 45, 46, 49 top right, 50, 53, 54 top, 56 bottom, 59 bottom right, 62, 66 all, 67, 68, 69 bottom left & right, 72 top, 73 top left, 74, 75, 78 top, 82, 83, 84 bottom, 86, 91 bottom, 92, 93 bottom, 94 left, 95 top & bottom, 96–97, 98–99, 100, 102 top, 104, 106 both, 108 bottom, 109 bottom, 110 all, 111 both; **Chad Slattery:** 69 top left; **Stokes Seed Co.:** 2, 12 bottom; **K. Bryan Swezey:** 108 top; **Michael S. Thompson:** 11 top right, 13 top left, 16–17, 18, 47, 64 bottom right, 107; **VISIONS-Holland:** 40 top & bottom, 48 left, 54 bottom right, 89; **Darrow M. Watt:** 41, 52 right, 76, 79, 94 right, 101 top, back cover middle; **Doug Wilson:** 15 bottom; **Tom Woodward:** 39 top left, 49 bottom, 51, 90 top; **Tom Wyatt:** 48 right.

5 6 7 8 9 QPD 04 03 02 01

CONTENTS

CONTAINERS
ONSTAGE

Picture your garden as a stage production, with yourself— the gardener—as the director. Your stage may be an expansive, big-as-Broadway country acre, or a single stairstep. Your production may be a carefully choreographed and sophisticated composition, or a whimsical, off-the-cuff effort. No matter what the size or style of your garden show may be, containers can be among your most versatile and reliable performers.

Sometimes container plantings are the stars, playing a dramatic solo role on a pedestal or by the front door, or appearing as a colorful grouped chorus at the edge of a patio. At other times they play supporting roles, making their appearance as a bright spot of color against a backdrop of green hedges, or as a foliage accent in the midst of an in-ground flower border.

As garden director, you can use containers in all sorts of creative ways. They may comprise your entire garden—a single box of annuals in a miniature "landscape" no bigger than a windowsill, or a whole collection of shrubs, trees, and flowers on a rooftop. As part of a larger, in-ground garden, cleverly placed containers can soften the edges between patio and lawn, screen a view, direct a visitor along a path, or extend a cheerful greeting at your door.

Nestled around and among the branches of a tree, birdhouses and pots of impatiens create a colorful village scene in miniature.

GO-ANYWHERE GARDENS

To one person, a container garden may be a single, glossy-leafed camellia in a prized ceramic urn by the front door. For another, it's a quirky collection of clay pots, planted higgledy-piggledy with annuals and succulents and clustered in a friendly jumble on a sunny patio. And for still another, it may be an arrangement of small trees, shrubs, and flowers that simulates an expansive in-ground garden.

For anyone, growing plants in pots yields twofold pleasure: the creative joy of putting together pots and plants in new and beautiful ways, and the challenge of placing them to best effect in and around the garden. Because containers are wonderfully versatile and relatively easy to move, they appeal to the part of us that likes to "fiddle around." You can hang them up or set them on a step, group them or isolate them, tuck them into an in-ground garden or set them out in glorious display on deck or patio. Use them to brighten a dull corner or soften a bare one, beckon a passerby into a shady nook or screen that nook from view. You can shift them seasonally to show them off at their best, and retire them when they fade.

Containers allow you to have a garden where there isn't any planting ground, or to grow favorite plants right up close to outdoor living areas, where you can really enjoy them. And if you have a woefully empty spot in a garden flower border, you can simply drop in a pot of colorful blooms.

ABOVE: A green garden border gains drama when an eye-catching container planting is set in its midst as a focal point. Here, a Japanese privet *(Ligustrum japonicum)* trained as a standard rises above garden sage from a plump pot of classic design. The colors and textures of plant and pot add a light, bright accent.

LEFT: A single, elegant ceramic container like this one, brimming with rosy begonias (two varieties) and fuchsias, can make a stunning statement anywhere you place it. The pot's shiny cobalt finish is a dramatic backdrop for the plants. Design: Jean Manocchio.

LEFT: A breezy collection of spring daffodils in clay pots, set about in clusters, helps to create a smooth transition between the yard and a step-up deck.

BELOW: Brilliant blue is the key to this design. The color-coordinated container pulls together plants and chairs into a cozy grouping.

ABOVE: This appealing stairstep grouping proves you don't need a big plot of earth to grow an abundant crop of vegetables. Colorful pots hold lettuces, herbs, tomatoes, and peppers.

RIGHT: A charming garden-in-miniature blooms in Chinese ceramic pots outside a window. Bright Martha Washington geraniums *(Pelargonium)* on a simple shelf can be enjoyed from both indoors and out.

SPACE-SHAPERS

Like rooms, stairs, and hallways in a house, truly interesting gardens often feature various distinctly defined areas within a larger plan. These might be places where people move or gather—seating areas, paths, entryways, even secret retreats. Or they might be beds or borders that create smaller spaces within the garden itself.

A pair of chairs beside a tub of succulents *(Sedum kamtschaticum)* offers an open invitation to pause and chat awhile. The foliage gives the setting a feeling of quiet intimacy; it's low enough that it's not a barrier, yet it affords a comfortable degree of separation. Design: Sue Moss.

You can enlist planted containers in lots of ways to help you shape and define such spaces. Set a lavishly planted barrel beside a pair of chairs, and—presto!—you have an intimate seating area. A row of matched pots seems to guide you along a walkway or lead you up a stairway. A pot of bright blooms beside a doorway clearly says "welcome."

Containers can provide pleasing transitions between spaces, too—between lawns and "hardscapes" such as patios, for example, or between the garden and a walkway. A pair of oversized pots at the edge of a walk ties paving and planting together, softening the look. A tub of plants at the edge of a deck or wide stairstep signals changing levels as well as seeming to anchor the space. And containers can serve as a buffer between public and private areas, as well. A couple of pots of bamboo or a potted bougainvillea espaliered against a trellis can create a real sense of privacy for a corner of your deck or patio.

TOP LEFT: Pots spilling over with blossoms usher the way through an ornate doorway into a lavishly planted and painted tableau, where an empty urn is a perfect focal point. Design: Rosemary Agostini.

BOTTOM LEFT: Marching up the steps and perched on the front stoop, potted succulents dress up simple brick stairs and lead the eye toward the porch. Plants and pots complement the quiet, earthy tones of the brick.

TOP RIGHT: A screen of foliage enfolds a tiny rooftop seating area and shields it from the surrounding hubbub. The profusion of flowering and foliage plants — all in pots — creates a serene hideaway. Design: Ken Druse.

BOTTOM RIGHT: What might be a rather pedestrian expanse of patio at the edge of a lawn becomes a charming outdoor room by virtue of container plantings positioned to define and soften its edges.

SPACE-MAKERS

Some homes don't seem to have space for any kind of garden at all. An apartment in a high-rise may have only a tiny balcony, or the house on the steeply sloping lot has no plantable ground. But such sites will accommodate containers—all-in-pots gardens that can be every bit as beautiful as their in-ground counterparts.

Decks and patios are prime candidates for container gardens. Balcony and rooftop container gardens can be particularly delightful surprises. These do require attention to practical considerations, such as wind and sun, and especially to weight. Large containers of plants can be very heavy, so it's important to place them over load-bearing areas of a structure and to plant in lightweight pots. And provisions should be made for catching excess water that may collect under them, to avoid damage to structures beneath.

Finally, don't forget to look up for places to plant. Wall pots, hanging baskets, window boxes, and boxes fastened to railings can create garden space where there didn't seem to be any—and contribute a lift of color and welcome greenery where you least expect to find it.

Within an intimate walled enclosure, plants in pots create a feast for the eyes at close range, while the larger garden beckons beyond the arched opening. Containers are arranged at varying levels to make a lovely self-contained patio garden.

RIGHT: Familiar red geraniums become dramatic when they echo the color of Adirondack-style garden chairs, transforming a wooden deck into a garden showplace.

BELOW: A bird's-eye view reveals the secret garden on this small deck—all in pots. A large mixed planting in a half-barrel fills in the corner; a variety of pots and plants lines the rail, and there's even a basket arrangement on the table.

ABOVE: It's a doorway into the sky—high-rise apartment extends out to a tiny balcony garden, where an arrangement of pots is punctuated by spiral-trained brush cherry *(Syzygium paniculatum)*.

LEFT: A porch becomes a garden when petunias, lobelia, geraniums, and periwinkle bloom from a window box that's anchored to the railing. Hanging planters provide yet more color.

SPOTLIGHT ON STYLE

When you give a beautifully planted container a starring role, it can make all the difference between a commonplace scene and a memorable one. Shelves and tables, pedestals and steps can be used to delightful effect to put your plants on display. At night, you can literally put pots in the spotlight by setting them under garden lights so their colors—even green foliage—are intensified. In the garden or on the patio, a large, dramatic pot can act as a focal point, drawing the eye into the scene. The pot itself can even function as a piece of garden sculpture.

The way you display your containers can also help establish your garden style. Like the people who create them, gardens have distinct personalities. Some have a casual, unplanned air, while others are meticulously laid out in formal fashion. A bright and frivolous arrangement gives one garden its cheery charm, while another is quietly serene and even a bit mysterious. You can develop a signature style with containers—or even in a single big container—just as you can with an in-ground garden.

Such classic styles as cottage, formal, minimalist, "natural," Italianate, or Japanese gardens can all be created and enhanced by plants in pots. Bright and cheerful annual flowers in wooden pots look just right in an informal setting. Beautifully shaped evergreens in ceramic jars enhance a Japanese-style garden, and the sculptural forms of cacti in clay pots carry out a spare, minimalist look. Every garden has its own special look, and there's a container planting that will work for any style.

ABOVE: A handsome wrought-iron rack brings this container collection up to eye level, framing the plants and giving them more importance than they would have if set out on the ground.

LEFT: Needlepoint ivy trained over a wire frame in a watering-can shape makes a witty garden statement.

Three container groupings demonstrate three different garden styles. ABOVE: A quiet, all-green garden artfully positions evergreens against slatted wood elements in a way that's reminiscent of a serene Japanese garden. Design: Laurence Ferar. RIGHT: Blue catmint, blue hibiscus, and lamb's ears are jumbled together in exuberant bouquets just the way they would be in a classic cottage garden border. BELOW LEFT: A few chrysanthemums in paper pulp pots and a couple of beloved antique milk cans create a little scene full of rustic charm.

LEFT: A pot overbrimming with succulents becomes a delightful sculptural focal point when it's anchored up on the wall.

BELOW: A chorus line of simple clay pots struts its stuff atop a ledge, nestled in the ivy as if the pots had grown there. The leafy background is an effective foil for bright blossoms.

PUBLIC IDEAS FOR PRIVATE PLACES

If imitation is the highest form of flattery, a stroll through city streets, civic centers, and even shopping centers can give you plenty of opportunities to flatter. Take a close look at public plantings—put together by garden professionals—for container gardening inspiration. What color schemes catch your eye? What plant combinations do you find especially appealing? How are arrangements changed with the seasons? The photographs on these two pages feature public areas in the West, where mild climates allow for year-round floral displays. Observe public plantings in your own region to see what works well for your climate zone.

OVERNIGHT IN A GARDEN

At Southern California's Seal Beach Inn, pictured below left, the passageways burst with flowering pots, container trees underplanted with blossoming plants, and hanging baskets of climbing roses. Wall-scaling bougainvillea and trumpet vines are trained to create niches for more pots and garden art. Varied heights help create depth and space to highlight showy annuals.

The inn's secret for continuous color is to "backplant" with seedlings so that something is coming into bloom as other plants fade. In spring, for example, ready-to-bloom nursery foxgloves are transplanted into big pots for immediate show. When their blooms wilt, they're transplanted to another area as something else takes over the spotlight.

SHOPPING BOUQUETS

At Stanford Shopping Center in Palo Alto, California, container bouquets make the most of walkways open to the outdoors. Annuals are planted in September and October to get plant roots going, and then tulip and daffodil bulbs are slipped among them in November and December. In January, anemones and ranunculus are planted from cell-packs.

A few tips for creating the big living bouquets that are the shopping center's signature:

- Include something bright—a little yellow, lime green, or iridescent white—to catch the eye.

- In late fall, cut back perennials, discarding easily replaced ones such as delphiniums and geraniums, if you wish. Move woody, deciduous ones (such as Russian sage) into cans until they leaf out again.

- A lot of perennials will bloom two or three times in mild climates if you cut them back. And don't be shy about cutting down annuals like petunias at midseason to get them to bush out again.

FAR LEFT: At the entrance, Seal Beach Inn guests are greeted with massed pots of seasonal color. Design: Dawn Pope.

LEFT: Fall-planted bouquet at Stanford Shopping Center holds pansies, pink stock, 'Ice Follies' daffodils, and 'Golden Parade' tulips. Design: Jackie Gray.

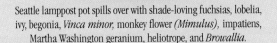

VICTORIA'S CONTAINER SECRETS

In Victoria, British Columbia, spectacular hanging baskets along the city's Inner Harbour have been delighting visitors for decades. Surprisingly, these baskets are not difficult to copy.

The lamppost baskets pictured below were planted with variegated nepeta, marigolds ('Lulu' and 'Gold Gem'), 'Shirley Claret' ivy geraniums, 'Angel Wings' schizanthus, lobelia ('Blue Fountain' and 'Sapphire Pendula'), 'Rose Madness' petunias, and a single *Lychnis coeli-rosa* (rose-of-heaven) each.

To recreate one of these planters, line a sturdy wire basket (16 inches across) with sphagnum moss and plant in layers, following the general directions on page 81. For the top, push a 2-inch by 4-foot strip of metal down 1 inch between moss and soil to form a circular collar. Fill with soil and plant the rose-of-heaven on top, surrounded by petunias and lobelia.

Keep your basket out of direct afternoon sun for a couple of weeks until plants are established.

Floral fireworks burst from Victoria baskets.

Seattle lamppost pot spills over with shade-loving fuchsias, lobelia, ivy, begonia, *Vinca minor*, monkey flower *(Mimulus)*, impatiens, Martha Washington geranium, heliotrope, and *Browallia*.

SEATTLE SUMMER

Amid the skyscrapers of downtown Seattle come summer, big pots of flowers stand out on sidewalks, bedeck corporate plazas, and hang from cast-iron pillars. To follow Seattle's example and turn a pot into a dramatic focal point, push plants close together so rootballs are about 2 inches apart. Cut back leggy shoots to encourage bushiness.

Most of Seattle's giant pots are rolled over on their sides once a year, emptied, and then filled with fresh potting mix. Controlled-release fertilizer is stirred in, and soil polymers are added so that pots can go longer between waterings. Seattle gardeners also use a special planting technique for hanging tubs. An aluminum pie pan is placed on top of the first 3 inches of potting soil in the bottom of the tub, and a handful of controlled-release fertilizer and a teaspoon of polymer is scattered into the pan—ensuring a layer of moist, nutrient-rich soil near plant roots.

POT

A garden-variety clay flowerpot or an antique oil jar, a wirework basket or a redwood tub, a faux stone bowl or even a clay flue tile—your choice of pots is every bit as important to the

ALL ABOUT
CONTAINERS

success of your container garden as are the plants themselves.

From the standpoint of looks, the container is half the picture—it's really a design element in itself. Plant a neatly shaped boxwood in a classic square Versailles tub, and you paint a picture of well-ordered formality. Or pot some succulents in a whimsical animal-shaped terra-cotta container, and you've created a quite different feeling—one of casual high spirits.

From a practical standpoint, a container must promote the health of the plants it holds as well as show them off to good effect. That means choosing a pot that will provide ample room for plant roots, good drainage, and the proper level of water retention.

In the following pages, you'll find practical advice both about matching plant needs to container size and material and about choosing pots that will make your plants look good. Let this chapter be your guide as you search for those special pots to be part of your own particular garden.

Pots, pots, and more pots—they come in a dazzling array of shapes, colors, and materials.
Shop for them at nurseries and home and garden centers, your local drugstore,
even flea markets and antique stores.

Cottage-garden–style arrangement pairs a charming terra-cotta basket with a subtly hued ceramic container.

DRILLING HOLES

If you've fallen for a container that has no drainage hole, you can probably drill one. Use an electric or hand drill for wood or plastic; for glazed or unglazed clay and concrete, use an electric drill with masonry or carbide bit.

If the pot's glaze is very thick, carefully chip through it using a hammer and nail (tap *very* lightly) before you begin drilling. For a medium-size container, a ½-inch hole is sufficient. For an extra-large container such as a half-barrel, drill four or five ¾-inch holes.

Support the pot upside down on a block of wood; to prevent cracking, drill with a small bit first, then increase the bit size until your hole is as big as you want. Adding a little water to the pot surface from time to time makes drilling easier.

BASIC CONSIDERATIONS

Sometimes you choose a container with a particular plant or group of plants in mind. At other times, a container chooses you—you fall for that gorgeous blue ceramic bowl or handmade, one-of-a-kind wooden window box. Later you'll figure out what to plant in it. Either way, your planting will be most successful if you follow a few simple guidelines—both stylistic and practical—when matching pot to plant.

WHAT'S YOUR STYLE?

The containers you choose will work best if they complement the style of your home and garden. Do you live in a shingled cottage-style home with an old-fashioned feel to the surrounding garden, or in an ultra-contemporary setting? The first might call for wooden window boxes and half-barrels, the latter for minimalist-style concrete containers.

Perhaps your home or garden has an Asian theme, perfect for classic Chinese ceramic. Or it might have a sunny Mediterranean feel, just right for elegant terra-cotta urns. Of course, if you feel confident about your design sense, you can go ahead and break the rules, mixing styles of containers as well as plantings for whimsical or dramatic effect.

When you match pot to plant, consider the impact they will have together. Will they make a bold, splashy statement or a small-scale, pastel picture? One good rule of thumb is this: If the pot is simple, the plants can dominate. But if the container is especially strong in character, you may want to keep the planting simple—a single rose, for example.

SHAPE AND SIZE

Pots and barrels, boxes, bowls, urns, and even attractive food tins—almost anything can be used as a plant container as long as it provides adequate drainage and has enough room for roots. Keep in mind a plant's expected shape and size at maturity when trying to figure out what shape and size of container are best. For example, a square box is suitable for a low, bushy azalea, while a tall tub fits a tapering boxwood.

Consider how fast your plants are likely to grow. Annuals probably won't outgrow their pots in one season. But do give both annuals and fast-growing perennials *some* room for growth. Slow-growing perennials, trees, and shrubs do best if moved in small steps, from year to year, into larger containers—each only a little larger than the previous one.

Pots are measured according to their top diameter. As a guideline, small pots (up to 8 inches) can be used for young plants and small types—dwarf annuals, for instance, and some succulents. Containers of about 8 to 12 inches are suitable for many flowering annuals and perennials, and for some shrubs and vines. Use bigger pots for larger shrubs and for bouquet-style plantings of annuals or perennials. Containers over 18 inches are the ones to choose for small trees and large shrubs, and to create a dramatic focal point or "anchor" planting.

Be aware that small pots generally require more maintenance than large ones of the same type—the soil in them tends to dry out more quickly, and they allow more fluctuation in temperature.

WHAT'S IT MADE OF?

A container may be made of almost anything; in fact, some of the most delightful ones weren't originally intended to be used for plants at all—see pages 28–29 for examples. But most commonly, containers are made of several main types of materials, and the ones you choose have an effect on your plants and what you need to do to take care of them.

In the following pages, you'll find information about the most common types of containers. When choosing among them, consider the climate and exposure in which you'll be using them, the plants you want, and the look you like. Your budget, the size you need, and how much time you're willing to spend watering will also affect your choice.

WATER, WATER

Perhaps the single most important practical consideration in choosing a container is how it affects the moisture in the soil it holds—and how that, in turn, affects the plants growing in it. Two factors are at work here: porosity and drainage.

POROSITY. Unglazed clay and paper pulp pots, untreated wood containers, and moss-lined wire baskets are all porous—made from materials that water and air can easily penetrate. This is good for plants, since roots develop best when they get plenty of oxygen. Soil in porous containers won't stay soggy after you water, because the pot walls absorb and evaporate excess moisture. And harmful salts don't build up around roots, since water and fertilizer migrate out through the container walls. *But* porosity also means that soil can dry out quickly, so you'll need to water frequently.

Nonporous containers, on the other hand, don't allow free passage of air and moisture. Glazed ceramic, plastic, fiberglass, concrete, and metal pots, and some treated or lined wood boxes, all fit this category. The soil in these containers tends to retain moisture, so you need to provide good drainage and avoid overwatering and overfeeding.

DRAINAGE. Poor drainage is a common cause of failure in container gardening. Fortunately, you can avoid this problem by using the right potting mix (see pages 98–99) and by planting in containers that efficiently drain off excess water.

For best results, a container needs to have at least one drain hole in the bottom. And any pot will benefit from being raised off the ground (see page 31).

NO DRAINAGE?

If you can't drill a drainage hole or are timid about doing so in a fragile or antique container, the best solution is to double-pot. Plant in a smaller, draining container that fits inside the one without a drain hole. Don't let the inner pot sit in water—empty any excess, or raise the smaller pot on a layer of pebbles.

Sleekly contemporary, corrugated steel culvert pipes form bottomless containers, inset in deck so they drain to the soil below.

TERRA-COTTA IS...

POROUS. Keeps soil from getting soggy but may necessitate frequent watering. Salts and minerals wick outward to collect on pot, not in soil—good for plant health but does cause white stains on pot.

HEAVY. Good for stability, as for a tree or in a windy location. But big pots, filled with soil, are hard to move, and too heavy for some rooftops and balconies.

FRAGILE. Even best quality can chip, crack, and break. Can crack in a freeze—move to protected spots in cold winters.

Square terra-cotta containers have a special elegance.

TERRA-COTTA POTS

Terra-cotta containers—those classic pots of clay—have been around for thousands of years, and they're still the favorites of gardeners the world over. For good looks, variety, and versatility, you can't beat them. And many gardeners say that plants just grow better in breathable terra-cotta.

Terra-cotta pots are unglazed clay, in colors ranging from the familiar brick red to less common buff or white shades. They come in every imaginable shape and size, from the ubiquitous mass-produced standard flowerpot to ornate one-of-a-kind creations. No matter what style of garden you have or what kind of plant you want to display, there's probably a terra-cotta pot that will fill the bill.

REVIVING A CLAY POT

Here's a trick to give an old terra-cotta pot a new patina. Remove as much crusting as possible with water and a stiff brush; let the pot dry for several hours. Then wipe a generous amount of linseed oil over the outside, using a soft cloth.

Let the pot sit for an hour or so. If the oil soaks in and the pot has dry patches, apply a second coat.

Not all clay pots are created equal. Least expensive—and least durable—are low-fired, mass-produced pots from Mexico, China, and Thailand. These are serviceable but break easily and may flake apart within a couple of years. Better-quality pots (many imported from Italy but some made in the United States, England, and Mexico) are fired at higher temperatures and last longer. At the high end of the scale are exquisite handmade containers being fashioned according to ancient models, largely in Italy—elegant olive jar shapes, for example, or tubs with surface embellishment of flower garlands or lions' heads. The pots shown at lower left—from Italy, Crete, and Spain—are examples.

How can you identify a quality pot? High-fired clay has a ring to it when you tap it with your knuckles, while a low-fired pot makes a dull thud. And touching a high-fired pot doesn't leave terra-cotta powder on your fingers. The surface of a low-fired pot can be easily scratched.

SHAPES AND SIZES

Standard clay flowerpots like the one shown immediately below—wider at the top, and at least as tall as they are wide—are shaped that way for a reason. Their tapering sides make plants easy to slide out, and their depth provides room for roots. Similarly-shaped fern pots, also called azalea pots, taper a bit less—they're three-quarters as high as they are wide. These are good for plants with shallow roots.

Specialty shapes and decorative treatments abound, from animal forms to strawberry pots (pocket planters) to long troughs with designs in relief. Bulb or seed pans are flat containers for growing shallow-rooted bulbs or succulents, starting seeds, and holding dish gardens.

PREPARING CLAY POTS

Low-fired types of clay pots may last longer if you paint the insides with asphalt roofing compound or paint inside and out with a clear vinyl sealer made for terra-cotta. (Adjust watering for the resulting loss of porosity.) You might also consider sealing your clay pots for water retention if you live in a dry climate.

Soak unsealed clay pots before planting to keep them from drawing moisture away from the soil.

CERAMIC—CLAY WITH A GLAZE

Glazed clay or ceramic pots come in almost any color, in a variety of forms—often in urn and bowl shapes. Their more finished appearance makes ceramic pots a strong design element in themselves. When choosing plants for them, make sure pot color harmonizes with foliage and flower colors, as well as with your garden style.

While glazed pots share many characteristics with their terra-cotta cousins, one important difference is that glazed pots are nonporous. They'll hold moisture longer, so it's important not to overwater or overfeed the plants you put in them.

SAVE THAT POT!

If a favorite clay pot breaks, don't despair—you can probably mend it. Use epoxy glue or fixture adhesive (neoprene mastic), following the manufacturer's directions. Work in a well-ventilated area and wear disposable gloves to keep glue off your hands.

Clean broken edges, apply glue, and assemble (you'll probably need a helper to hold the pieces together). While the glue dries, keep pieces bound together by using rope, nylon cord, or wire for big pots, masking tape for small ones.

While the glue is wet, scrape off any extra that has oozed onto the outside of the pot. After the glue is dry, sandpaper off excess glue—this smooths the surface and also colors in the cracks on unglazed pots.

Handsomely crafted planters keep bamboo, naturally rampant, under control for use as a living screen.

A wooden tub is the perfect container for a casual mixed planting of rainbow-colored annuals.

WOOD BOXES AND TUBS

Naturally at home in garden settings, wood can be used to fashion containers in sizes, shapes, and styles to fit all sorts of spaces and garden designs. And it's durable and easy to maintain. No wonder wood is a popular choice for container gardens.

Most wood containers have a casual or even rustic look; a half-barrel, for example, looks appealing planted with bright annuals or a mixed selection of vegetables and flowers. But other wood containers can lend a more formal look to the garden, especially if they have decorative details or are painted to harmonize with architectural elements.

Wood is often the best choice to hold a tree or shrub—big wood containers tend to be less expensive than same-sized terra-cotta, and not quite as heavy.

Although a container can be built from almost any kind of wood, those made of rot-resistant redwood, cedar, or cypress are the longest-lasting. And whether wood containers look rough-and-ready or have a smooth finish, the sides and bottom should be at least ⅞-inch thick for good insulation. Joints should be tight and water retentive, put together with galvanized screws or nails to prevent rusting. If staves are held together with metal bands, the bands should be rustproof, or they'll need painting with rust-retarding paint.

When buying a half-barrel, try to find one that's been stacked upside down (this helps keep bands from slipping). Look for staves that fit tightly.

SHAPES AND SIZES

From barrels to boxes, wood containers come both plain and fancy. Long, narrow planters are useful on window sills, against walls or fences, or along paths. Versailles boxes, painted or natural, are modeled on classic containers from formal gardens of historical palaces and stately homes. They have four feet and decorative corner knobs.

Tubs may be round or hexagonal. Half-barrels are sawed from oak barrels originally used to hold whiskey or wine. They are usually more moderately priced than other wood containers, and their thick wood provides good insulation and holds up well.

Some wood boxes are cleated—strips of lumber are attached to the bottom, providing fingerhold space for moving the container and also allowing air to circulate beneath.

PREPARING WOOD CONTAINERS

For containers held together with metal bands, you can remove any rust with steel wool, a wire brush, or a drill with wire brush attachment. Coating the bands with an oil-base rust-retarding paint will help keep them rust-free. (You can use any color, but black changes the pot's appearance the least.)

To keep bands from slipping down on a half-barrel or other container that tapers inward, you can drive in galvanized nails with wide heads just under the bottom edges of the bands.

If you wish, you can prolong the life of your container by sealing the inside as described below. And, if you want a particular look, you can apply stain, clear wood finish, or paint to the outside. If you use paint, you'll probably need to apply a new coat from time to time. Keep in mind that any finish that waterproofs a pot also makes it water-retentive—adjust your watering accordingly.

All wood containers will last longest if air can circulate underneath. You can place the container on a dolly (for mobility) or nail wooden blocks or strips (cleats) to the bottom before filling with soil. (See page 31 for other ways to raise pots.)

Begonias and fuchsias thrive in a simple trough suitable for setting on a ledge or edging a path or patio.

TO SEAL OR NOT TO SEAL?

Wood containers, even those made of rot-resistant cedar or redwood, will last longer if you coat the insides with a sealing compound before planting. But that also does away with wood's natural porosity—the quality that lets air and water move freely through container walls. So is it a good idea or not?

Your answer may depend on what kind of wood you're dealing with (redwood and cedar last a very long time even without being treated), your climate, and the plants you want to grow.

Porous pots promote healthy root growth but require more watering. Does your climate make moisture-retentive (nonporous) containers a reasonable choice? Are the plants you want thirsty or drought-resistant?

If you do choose to seal containers, paint the insides with a nontoxic sealer such as asphalt roofing compound (available at hardware stores) or asphalt emulsion used for sealing pruning cuts (available at nurseries or garden centers). Never use creosote—it will harm plants.

Another option is to line the container with heavy-duty (4- to 6-mil) plastic. Punch holes to match the container's drainage holes, then trim away any overhang at the top, tuck in the edges neatly around the top, and staple in place.

Few plants do well if their roots sit in soggy soil, so if you seal containers, take care not to overwater. The same goes for feeding, since fertilizer won't be flushed out as readily as with porous pots.

NO HANDS!

Here's a tip to make a pot-painting project easier. Set the container you're painting on top of a can and you'll be able to rotate the pot without touching it.

CONTAINER ART

Pots for your plants can be as wildly hued and patterned as a circus, or as sedate as an old-fashioned afternoon tea party. Here are two distinct directions you can take to transform ordinary pots into pieces of garden art.

With either method, the pots are coated with a waterproof sealer. Plants growing in them won't need watering as frequently as those in unsealed clay or wood pots. Be sure your painted pots are completely dry before planting in them.

Design: Françoise Kirkman

PAINTED POTS

Here's a quick and easy project that gives your creative powers free rein. Use either a clay pot or a wood container (sanded first), and choose designs and colors to complement the plant that will be at home in the pot. Look for the materials at a hardware store. Here's how to proceed:

1 Coat the pot inside and out with waterproofing, and let dry thoroughly (a day or more).

2 Coat the inside of the pot with roofing compound, stopping within 2 inches of the pot rim.

3 Use a roller to paint a base coat on the outside of the pot; let dry.

4 Then go creative, using a brush and sponges to apply paint designs to your pot and perhaps a matching saucer. Here are some ideas:

- Paint on freehand swirls or zigzags, or use masking tape to define geometric shapes as you paint.

- Create simple outlines, such as birds, leaves, and flowers.

- Cut a square, triangle, or circle from a sponge and use it to stamp on patterns.

- Spatter-paint by coating a brush with paint and flicking it onto the pot.

MATERIALS

Water-based nontoxic water-proofing
Roofing compound
Latex paints for base coat and designs
Paintbrush, roller, sponges

COLOR-WASHED "FAUX" POTS

This project turns the centuries-old art of "faux-painting" into a pot-decorating technique. Depending on your choice of colors, you can make terra-cotta look like plaster with moss growing on it, or make cement look like aged terra-cotta! "Faux" just means fake—but the results are rich-looking, even if they are fakes.

You can use almost any unglazed pot—inexpensive clay flowerpots or more ornate containers in clay or concrete. Paint stores sell all the required materials except the acrylic paint, available at art supply stores. The amounts listed will cover at least four pots.

Follow these steps, adjusting the degree of coverage for each color to create the look you want. For a less uniform look, blot paint lightly in some areas and more heavily in others. For a more solid appearance, brush on more color and blot lightly all over.

1 Coat inside of the pot with waterproofing and let dry completely (a day or more).

2 Cut cheesecloth into 1½-foot lengths, wash with dishwashing soap, rinse, and hang to dry (do not use a clothes dryer).

3 Brush cream-colored exterior paint on the outside and about 1½ inches down the inside of the pot. Let dry thoroughly, about 3 hours.

4 In a plastic container, mix 1 part (¼ cup) first color of paint, 1 part (¼ cup) low-luster sealer, and 2 parts (½ cup) water. Starting at the top, apply with a paintbrush, using a scrunched-up piece of cheesecloth to blot drips, until base coat is covered. Let dry for 3 hours.

5 Apply second color, using the same proportions as in previous step and blotting drips with cheesecloth. Remove more or less of the paint as you go, depending on how dense you want the color. Let dry for 3 hours.

6 For third color, squeeze acrylic paint onto a plate (or use latex), then dip a clean brush first into the paint and then into water. Brush onto pot, letting paint drip down. Blot to spread the color, or let some drips remain. Let dry thoroughly.

Design: Io Bonini

MATERIALS

1 quart water-based nontoxic waterproofing
1 quart cream-colored exterior latex paint
1 quart *each* latex paint in two other colors
1 quart low-luster paint sealer
2-ounce tube acrylic paint in burnt-umber,
   or 1 quart similar-colored latex paint
Paintbrushes
5 yards cheesecloth

WHICH COLORS?

Try one of these approaches when choosing colors for a color-washed pot:

- Take a favorite piece of fabric to the paint store and match the colors.

- Use colors that complement one another—such as apricot, green, and burnt umber.

- Use colors that complement the plants that will grow in the pot.

Experiment with color combinations on watercolor paper until you get the look you want. You can blow-dry the paper with a hair dryer to speed up the process.

MORE POT CHOICES

Although terra-cotta and wood containers dominate the field, you can find pots made out of lots of other materials, too. Some are easy to track down at any nursery or garden center, while others take a bit more searching. Specialty mail-order catalogs are a good source for some of the less common kinds. You can also ask to look through suppliers' catalogs at a nursery—the nursery may be willing to special-order containers for you.

FIBERGLASS

Do you want the look of classic stone or terra-cotta urns and troughs—complete with designs like swags and flowers in relief—without the weight of stone or terra-cotta? Take a look at the fiberglass and resin pots on the market today.

These containers are showing up in catalogs, nurseries, and specialty shops, and they're often hard to distinguish from the "real thing" until you actually touch them. Their colors may mimic the gray of stone or the white, buff, or red of terra-cotta. Although some are inexpensive, some are as costly as the best terra-cotta containers.

PLASTIC

Plastic containers are available nearly everywhere, in a wide variety of colors, styles, shapes, and sizes—from the humble pots in which nursery plants come home to fancier terra-cotta lookalikes. And plastic containers are less expensive than almost any other pots of comparable size.

If you don't like the looks of plastic but don't want to transplant, slip nursery pots inside more decorative ones. Or make the pot "wraps" shown on page 27.

PAPER PULP

Made of compressed, recycled paper, pulp pots may not be beautiful but will blend in with a casual or rustic garden—especially if plants spill over the edges. They're a good choice for one-season plantings of vegetables, and for large-scale temporary plantings when another kind of pot might be too expensive. Pulp containers are the least expensive on the market.

Fiberglass urn

Plastic pot

Paper pulp pot

CONCRETE, METAL, AND WIRE

Containers made of concrete, metal, or wire mesh can be old-fashioned or ultra-modern in style.

CAST CONCRETE is a durable choice for a large, permanent container. The thick, nonporous walls may be heavily pebbled (aggregate) or smooth, the styling contemporary or classical. Generously-sized concrete containers are perfect for mature shrubs, small trees, and extravagant "bouquets."

METAL CONTAINERS of iron, brass, and copper show up in antique shops, and copies of ornate 19th-century cast-iron urns are offered in some garden catalogs. In time, oxidation can give a metal pot the look of its antique prototype. Metal containers are most often used as cachepots—to show off plants already planted in other containers.

Metal absorbs heat—keep containers out of hot sun to avoid damage to roots. Protect the surfaces they rest on, since metal can "sweat."

WIRE POTS are usually found in the form of mesh hanging baskets or wall planters (see pages 30–31). Fancier types may feature coated wire or special shapes.

PLASTIC POT DRESS-UPS

Those homely plastic pots that nurseries use for gallon-size and larger plants are anything but attractive. But you don't necessarily have to transplant the plants you bring home in them. You can make a "pot wrap" that lets you to use the original containers but keep them out of sight at the same time. And you can easily switch pots as your favorite plants come into bloom.

Although they look like regular soil-filled containers with bottoms, these cover-ups are actually sleeves that simply go around the pots. Some garden centers also carry manufactured versions of pot cover-ups.

The bottomless boxes shown at right are made of ¾-inch exterior plywood faced with wood strips to give them a finished look. The taller one in the background is 15 inches high, the smaller one 7½ inches. The walls are butt-joined, equal-size rectangles, fastened with galvanized nails. Mitered 1 by 3s were nailed on to form the top lips.

The foreground box, which will hold four 1-gallon pots, has ⅜-by 1½-inch lath nailed to its sides. Waterproof exterior vinyl paint was used to cover the box and lath strips.

The more rustic-looking background box, for a single 5-gallon pot, has green-stained pieces of fir glued to its sides with waterproof wood glue. The fir pieces were ripped from a 2 by 4 in random widths and thicknesses.

ANYTHING-GOES PLANTERS

There's plenty of room to cut loose a little when choosing containers for your plants. Finding a wonderful one-of-a-kind container may be pure serendipity—you're wandering around a flea market or exploring a shop's dusty back corner and see that forgotten jug or funny old tin. Sometimes just looking at something in a new way results in a "new" container—people have been known to plant flowers in old boots!

Almost anything goes—wheelbarrows and cookie tins, pails, bushel baskets, even hollowed-out logs or pockets in rocks. The only requirements are enough space for plant roots and adequate drainage. And keep in mind whether the container is made of a porous or nonporous material, since that will affect your watering schedule.

If what you've chosen doesn't have a drainage hole, see page 18 for help in drilling one. With some containers, such as an olive oil can or other food tin, you can simply punch holes in the bottom with a nail. (Metal tins are likely to "sweat" moisture, so protect the surfaces on which they rest.) Alternatively, simply set a pot that has a drainage hole inside the container without one.

TOP: An old tree stump gets a new life as planter for ivy, impatiens, and ferns.

ABOVE: Chimney pipes come out into the garden as pots for herbs. Dirt and gravel in the bottom of the pipes gives them stability.

LEFT: Succulents share a kitchen colander.

TOP: This venerable wheelbarrow functions as a mobile planter; it's leaky enough to provide good drainage.

LEFT: Don't throw away that broken pot! An elegant terra-cotta fragment, laid on its side, is a fine home for a cache of petunias.

ABOVE: A decorative olive oil tin houses a fuchsia.

CONTAINERS ALOFT

Whether they're baskets of bright annuals and trailing vines dancing beneath a porch roof or pocket pots spilling over with flowers against a sunny wall, containers brought up to eye level give a whole new dimension to outdoor living spaces. Raising plants lets you enjoy every detail of flowers and foliage. And a hanging plant can block an undesirable view, screen sunlight, create a pleasing picture outside a window, or break up a stark expanse of wall.

Lobelia paints a dainty picture spilling from an elegant moss-lined wire basket.

PLANTS OVERHEAD

Suspended by chains or wires, hanging planters may be made of wire, terra-cotta, glazed ceramic, wood, or plastic.

WIRE BASKETS—or baskets made of coated metal strips—are open all around. Plants can be inserted at top, sides, and bottom (see page 81) so that eventually the basket is covered in flowers and foliage.

These baskets drain freely and require lots of watering—often more than once a day in warm weather. They aren't suitable for hot climates or spots exposed to lots of sun or wind. And be careful to hang them where water staining won't be a problem on the surface below.

WOOD PLANTERS are good alternatives to wire baskets in spots where they'll be exposed to drying winds and sun. They have rustic charm when planted with a combination of bright flowers and trailing plants so that at least part of the container is visible. See page 23 for ways of making wood more moisture-retentive.

TERRA-COTTA AND CERAMIC POTS can be heavy, so be sure to hang them securely from a sturdy support. Unglazed terra-cotta can dry out quickly—keep on top of watering. Glazed ceramic retains moisture longer.

PLASTIC POTS are good for hanging because they're lightweight and don't allow soil to dry out as quickly as some types. They often come with their own saucers for catching drips. You can encourage plants to spill out over the sides and conceal a plastic pot, so its looks aren't as much of an issue as they might be elsewhere.

HANGING THEM

Containers made for hanging come with holes or hooks in the rim and often a hanger as well. Other containers can be adapted for overhead use with the addition of a hanger; add screw eyes to the rim of a wood container or fit clip-on wire hangers over the rim of a terra-cotta or plastic pot.

Use strong galvanized wire or chain for hanging. Make sure hooks are sturdy, and hook them over a strong support or suspend from sturdy lag-thread clothesline hooks or screw eyes. Swivels in the hanging apparatus will let you rotate the pot for even exposure to sunlight.

Choose a hanging location that satisfies the plants' growth requirements *and* offers enough support for the container. And be sure pots hang where nobody's likely to bump into them.

ON THE WALL

In Mexico and the Mediterranean, centuries-old walls covered with pots create almost magical vertical gardens. You can borrow this idea by using specially-made flat-backed wall containers or adapting regular clay or ceramic pots with clips or holders.

WIRE WALL BASKETS are "half-basket" versions of the ones used for hanging overhead. A swankier cousin is the so-called reproduction "hayrack"—made of heavier vertical strips of metal. Both types can be planted top, sides, and bottom (see page 81).

WOOD AND CLAY WALL POTS are planted only from the top. Clay wall pots may be glazed or unglazed; the latter will dry out more quickly.

REED OR WICKER BASKETS can make attractive wall containers, too. Line them with plastic to make them last longer and hold water better (see page 90).

ATTACHING THEM

Avoid walls exposed to drying winds, long periods of hot summer sun, or heavy shade. Be sure the wall or fence is strong enough to support the weight of filled pots and won't be damaged by water from the pots.

Geranium blossoms glow against a color-washed wall.

Most wall pots come with holes or brackets for screws or hooks. To use regular round clay pots as wall pots, purchase metal clips to attach to their rims.

Ask at a hardware store for the appropriate attaching hardware for your wall surface. Many people fasten wire baskets directly against the wall; others like to provide for some air circulation behind them. To do so, leave a slight space between the container and the wall when you screw it in place; or use heavy-duty staples to attach a wood block to the basket back.

OFF THE GROUND

One way to promote good drainage and air circulation in container plantings—and prevent water stains on decks and patios—is to lift the containers up off the ground. Put bricks, wood blocks, or purchased "feet" beneath pots, nail cleats onto wood containers, or use pots with built-in feet. Water can then run freely—and the increased air circulation keeps water from staining surfaces and slows the decay of wood and paper pulp pots. A final advantage: insect pests are less likely to set up housekeeping beneath raised pots.

Providing drip saucers or trays is even more effective at keeping water off deck and patio surfaces, but be sure to empty saucers so soil doesn't stay soggy. Coat the insides of unglazed clay or other porous saucers with asphalt roofing emulsion or other waterproof sealer to prevent seepage.

Shown here is a selection of trivets and pot feet available at nurseries and garden centers. To make cleats for wooden

containers that don't already have them, nail strips of 1- by 2-inch lumber across box bottoms, inset at both ends.

Container gardening gives you a golden opportunity to experiment with a wide range of plants on a manageable scale. You can grow a rainbow of flowers, a whole array of vines, shrubs, and trees—even many edibles— all in pots.

CHOOSING YOUR
PLANTS

Broadly speaking, almost any plant can live in a container for a while. But you want every plant you put in your pots to really pull its weight in terms of color, shape, and style. It also makes sense to choose the plants that will perform most reliably in the confines of a container. With the right plants, a reasonable amount of attention will yield highly satisfying results.

So although the selection of suitable container plants may seem vast, certain plants are proven star performers. You'll find a sampling of favorites in this chapter along with general guidelines on choosing good container plants. Annuals, perennials, and bulbs offer a wealth of possibilities for flower lovers, some repeating over quite a few growing seasons and others providing an exciting but fleeting burst of color. Vines are a good choice when you want a leafy natural screen or a bit of greenery to soften a wall. And if you need a solid foundation for your pot garden—and perhaps a touch of drama—you can choose a shrub or small tree.

Plants suitable for containers run the gamut from flowering annuals and perennials to shrubs and small trees—even flowering plants trained to treelike form as standards, like the one at right.

SHOPPING GUIDE

You're in your local nursery, surrounded by a dazzling array of plants—annuals in flower, trees, climbing vines, and much, much more. Which should you choose to plant in your containers? Are the criteria different from those you use to select plants for an in-ground garden? The answer is yes—and no.

Most good advice regarding plant selection for the garden can be equally well applied to choosing container plants. But there are some special considerations to keep in mind.

Your local nursery is likely to inspire that "kid-in-a-candy-store" feeling with its colorful selection of plants; your job is to choose wisely.

WHAT WILL WORK?

Almost any plant can live in a container for a while. But what characteristics distinguish a really outstanding container plant?

Success depends largely on taking into account the restrictions that container life puts on a plant. A container—even a large one—is a self-contained environment: a kind of closed system that restricts a plant's space as well as the amount of water and nutrients it receives. In addition, plants in pots are often on display in a more focused way than they might be in-ground, making them subject to closer attention.

For these reasons, you'll want to select plants whose growth habits and requirements are suited to a container environment. You'll also want to choose plants that offer maximum eye appeal—color, form, texture, or all three. Such plants will deliver the most enjoyment for the amount of care they require.

Side by side, a lemon tree and a purple-flowered clematis vine are good container choices from two distinctive plant categories.

Look for plants that have these characteristics:

- Naturally compact growth habit
- Long (or repeat) flowering season
- Attractive foliage
- Multiple interest—flowers, attractive foliage, berries, autumn leaf color

Conversely, to get the most out of your container garden, *avoid* plants that have these characteristics:

- Straggly growth habit
- Vigorous climbing or spreading habit (unless you are willing to prune heavily)
- Short flowering season
- Lackluster foliage
- Greedy, dense root system
- Water-guzzling demands
- Very large size when mature

Annuals are the exception to these "rules"—since they only live for a season, you can choose just about any kind, so long as it's not such a rampant grower it will outgrow its pot in a season, or so thirsty it will need a lot of extra watering.

Of course, you may choose your container plants for a variety of reasons. Maybe you want to grow tropical plants (such as many orchids) that can only stay outdoors for a short period in your area, and containers will let you move them come cold weather. Or you may opt for plants with special requirements—like acid-loving camellias or rhododendrons—that won't grow in your garden soil. Perhaps you want to grow edibles but don't have in-ground space. Or maybe you *enjoy* coddling plants and don't mind if the ones you pick will need extra attention.

CONSIDER THE CONDITIONS

When you are plant-shopping, keep in mind your general climate conditions, as well as the particular conditions in your yard or on your patio, deck, or balcony. Your local nursery will usually carry only those plants that thrive in your area. But double-check by talking with knowledgeable nursery staff or by reading about specific plants in a source such as Sunset's *National Garden Book* or *Western Garden Book*. Be aware of a plant's potential special needs, such as protection from frost, special soil or nutrients, exposure, and so forth. Can you meet those needs?

The mini-environment of yard, patio, or balcony has its own particular conditions. It may be shady or sunny, windy or still; the air may tend to be cool and moist, or hot and dry. The container itself is part of this mini-environment. Some pots (like terra-cotta) are highly porous and allow quick evaporation of moisture; plants will do best in these pots if they don't need lots and lots of water. Other containers (such as plastic) keep the soil damp longer, so they're better for moisture-loving plants than for plants that like drier soil. To find out about the properties of various types of pots, read "All about Containers," starting on page 17.

Usually you'll find exposure needs listed for each kind of plant at the nursery. Look for plants that will prosper under the conditions you have to offer. Some plants love full sun, some can take either full or part sun, some do best in partial shade, and some need deep shade.

PLANT CATEGORIES

Annuals, perennials, and bulbs . . . trees, shrubs, and vines. What *kinds* of plants will you choose? Do you want a display that's more or less permanent, varying little from season to season? Then you'll want to choose shrubs, vines, small trees, or perennial plants that can live in a container for a long time and respond well to pruning, shaping, and dividing.

Or do you want instant color—either to dress up your patio for a party or to provide a summer's-worth of bright flowers and fragrance? You'll want to choose annuals—flowering plants that live only for a single growing season.

What you're looking for may well be a combination of these approaches. You might select perennial plants and shrubs for interesting texture, foliage, and flowers over several seasons and put them together with a changing assortment of annuals and bulbs for additional shows of color. Your combination could be in a single pot or in a grouping of pots.

Read the rest of this chapter for guidelines on choosing good container plants within the various plant categories, from annuals to trees to herbs.

STARTING FROM SEED

If you have the time, you can save money by starting many plants from seed—especially annuals, most herbs, many vegetables, and salad greens. Nurseries and garden catalogs offer a wide selection, some of which you probably won't find in seedling form. For best results, use seeds packed for the current year (check the date stamped on the seed packet).

Some seeds, like the sweet peas pictured below, do best if soaked for a few hours before planting to soften their coats. Sow seeds into containers filled with a moistened lightweight potting soil mix, following packet directions. Cover with a thin layer of equal parts soil mix and sand; keep pots shaded and soil moist. When seedlings are a few inches tall, move pots to give plants the light they need; thin seedlings to 4 to 6 inches apart. Start fertilizing 4 weeks or so later.

Perennials like these coreopsis plants are most often offered for sale by nurseries in cell-packs (at left in photo), 4-inch pots, and gallon-sized containers.

SIZE AND FORM

In the nursery, you'll find plants in various sizes and forms. When choosing among them, even if you're shopping for a tree, go by this rule of thumb: *smaller is usually better.* Why? Because healthy plants in small containers, if not rootbound, generally go through less transplant shock and get established faster than larger plants. And you'll get a longer season of bloom if you buy plants before they flower—though nonbloomers may be hard to find. Smaller plants usually give you better value for your money; just keep in mind how big the plant will eventually get, since it may fill up its container quite quickly.

Availability of the following plant forms may vary from region to region.

BEDDING PLANTS, mainly annuals, are flowering plants that you buy for a display of color. They're available in cell-packs (also called six-packs and pony packs) of six 1-inch-wide cells; jumbo packs (or color packs) of six 2½-inch-wide cells; 4-inch pots; 1-gallon containers; and 8-inch pulp pots. Annuals are also sometimes sold in undivided flats of 64 or 81 plants, or in half-flats.

PERENNIALS usually are sold in cell-packs, jumbo packs, 4-inch pots, and 1-gallon containers.

TREES, SHRUBS, AND VINES come in plastic, metal, or pulp containers in 1-, 2-, 5-, and 7-gallon sizes, or larger.

BARE-ROOT deciduous trees, shrubs, vines, and some perennials are available in nurseries in the winter and spring, depending on your climate zone, and often through mail-order catalogs as well.

BALLED-AND-BURLAPPED shrubs and trees are sold with a ball of soil wrapped around their roots in burlap (or synthetic burlap), tied with twine. The appearance of B-and-B plants at the nursery signals that their planting time has arrived in your area.

BULBS are available seasonally from nurseries and mail-order catalogs.

HEALTHY PLANTS

No plant, no matter how well-suited to your garden, will grow successfully if it doesn't start out in good condition. Look for compact plants with good leaf color. Leaves should be perky, not limp and wilted. Avoid straggly or crowded plants. Large container plants such as trees should be well-branched, with healthy-looking bark and foliage.

Avoid plants that are rootbound—look at the bottom of the container for evidence of roots. Conversely, you'll sometimes find seedlings that were planted into cell-packs or 4-inch pots too soon and are underdeveloped. If the leaves of the plant extend to the container edge, the plant is mature enough to transplant.

Choose bare-root plants that have plump, fresh-looking roots. Slightly dried roots may revive if you soak them in water overnight before planting, but there's no cure for really withered ones.

Avoid plants that look like these! The snapdragon at left is dried out, the delphinium in the center is suffering from overwatering, and the campanula at right is too small for its pot.

THE WHOLE PICTURE

When you walk through the nursery, keep in mind the colors and textures that different flowers and foliage can provide. Look for plant shapes that are pleasing in themselves or that will help create a successful container arrangement. For guidelines on choosing and combining colors, shapes, and textures, read "Great Container Designs," beginning on page 61.

Sweet pea

SWEET SCENTS FOR POTS

When you shop for plants, you might want to consider more than just the way they look. Some plants create a drift of fragrance that gives an extra dimension to your container garden. Whether it's the scent of night jessamine wafting through your bedroom window or the sweet surprise you get when you lean over to sniff a miniature tree rose, fragrance can be a potent pleasure when it's offered close at hand by container plants.

A plant's fragrance—nature's way of encouraging pollinators to come close—may be in its flowers, its foliage, or both. Most flowers have the strongest scent in warm, humid weather. From foliage, you'll get the sharpest whiff, regardless of the weather, by touching the leaves.

Here are a few wonderfully fragrant plants—vines, trees, annuals, perennials, shrubs, and bulbs—to sniff out for planting in containers:

Angel's trumpet (*Brugmansia***)**
Citrus trees
English lavender (*Lavandula angustifolia***)**
Flowering tobacco (*Nicotiana alata* 'Grandiflora'**)**
Freesia
Gardenia
Heliotrope (*Heliotropium arborescens***)**
Hyacinth
Juniper
Lily
Lily-of-the-valley (*Convallaria majalis***)**
Mexican orange (*Choisya ternata***)**
Narcissus
Night jessamine (*Cestrum nocturnum***)**
Peony
Rose
Star jasmine (*Trachelospermum jasminoides***)**
Stock (*Matthiola incana***)**
Sweet alyssum (*Lobularia maritima***)**
Sweet pea (*Lathyrus odoratus***)**
Winter daphne (*Daphne odora***)**

ANNUALS

Sunny yellow marigolds, scarlet zinnias, and frilly pink petunias—when you think of color for your containers, you naturally think of annuals.

Annuals—those plants that complete their life cycle in one growing season—are especially rewarding to plant in containers. Because they're short-lived plants that you can buy at reasonable prices or even start from seed, you can feel free to experiment with them— to try various kinds and combinations. If you don't like the results, replacing them isn't too daunting.

There are lots of ways to "play" with annuals. You can:

- Buy annuals in bloom and pot them for almost instant color, for a patio party or other special event, or just for a spring or summertime lift.

- Use annuals to experiment with color. Try a combination of hot, bright colors, or a soft pastel medley. Come up with some surprise combinations—like red and purple *Salvia splendens* with pink and magenta verbena. Or try using only foliage color, mixing coleus with dusty miller and maybe purple-leafed 'Dark Opal' basil.

- Plant an all-annuals pot and keep it blooming all summer by replacing any spent plants with new ones that are just coming into bloom.

- Use annuals as blooming fillers in a pot with one or more perennials or a shrub, vine, or small tree; they'll provide plenty of color while the permanent plants are filling out or after they've finished their bloom season.

WHICH ONES?

With good potting soil and attentive care, almost any annual will grow and bloom successfully in a container. But those that provide the most color and longest bloom will give you the greatest return for their cost in effort as well as money. The lists on the facing page include some reliable favorites; also see "Vines," pages 48–49, for annuals that you can train to climb onto a trellis.

Some perennials that only survive winter in the mildest climates are often grown as annuals. Petunias, for example, are really perennials in frost-free regions. Even so, gardeners generally treat them as annuals, starting with new plants each year.

Choose young plants not yet in bloom, or just starting to bloom, unless you're looking for instant color; these will per-

A drift of vibrant multihued coleus in pots demonstrates that not only flowers can provide stunning color.

form best in the long run. When selecting annuals to share a container, make sure they have similar exposure and watering requirements.

PLANTING TIPS

Annuals fall into two main categories: *cool-season or hardy annuals*, which bloom in spring or fall (and even winter in mild climates); and *warm-season annuals*, the summer bloomers.

In cold-winter climates, plant cool-season annuals in early spring, as soon as frost danger has passed. Plant warm-season annuals later, when the weather has warmed up. In mild-winter climates, plant cool-season annuals very early in the spring or even in the fall to get the most springtime bloom (some will even bloom in winter). Warm-season annuals may start appearing in nurseries as early as February in warm-climate areas. Late summer is the time to plant fall-blooming cool-season annuals.

When you plant them, space annuals an average of 4 to 6 inches apart in the pot. Most container-grown annuals require regular water and frequent fertilizer applications (every 2 weeks) to keep them at peak bloom as long as possible.

To start annuals from seed, see page 36.

Lathyrus odoratus

FAVORITE CONTAINER ANNUALS

20 SUMMER ANNUALS

Begonia, bedding*
Catharanthus roseus
    (Madagascar periwinkle)*
Celosia (cockscomb)
Centaurea cineraria (dusty miller)*
Coleus hybridus (coleus)*
Convolvulus tricolor (dwarf morning glory)
Coreopsis tinctoria (annual coreopsis, calliopsis)
*Impatiens**
Lobelia erinus (annual lobelia)
Lobularia maritima (sweet alyssum)
Nicotiana alata (flowering tobacco)*
Petunia hybrida (common garden petunia)*
Phlox drummondii (annual phlox)
Portulaca grandiflora (rose moss)
Salvia splendens (scarlet sage)*
Senecio cineraria (dusty miller)*
Tagetes (marigold)
Tropaeolum majus (garden nasturtium)
*Verbena hybrida**
Zinnia

10 COOL-WEATHER ANNUALS

Antirrhinum majus (snapdragon)*
Brassica (flowering cabbage/kale)
*Calendula officinalis**
Lathyrus odoratus (sweet pea)
Matthiola incana (stock)*
Myosotis sylvatica (forget-me-not)
Papaver nudicaule (Iceland poppy)*
Primula malacoides (fairy primrose)
Senecio hybridus (cineraria)
Viola (johnny jump-up, pansy, viola)*

5 ANNUALS FOR GREAT FOLIAGE COLOR

Begonia, bedding*
Brassica (flowering cabbage/kale)
Centaurea, Senecio cineraria (dusty miller)*
Coleus hybridus (coleus)*
Impatiens, New Guinea hybrids*

*Perennials often grown as annuals

TOP: Rosy petunias keep company with yellow-faced pansies in a rustic half-barrel.

BOTTOM: For something a little different for mild-winter areas, plant a mixed bouquet of intensely colored ornamental cabbages and kales *(Brassica)*. Design: Rick LaFrentz.

Lily-of-the-Nile plants *(Agapanthus)* raise floral globes in two colors.

PERENNIALS

Many people think of perennials—those plants that grow and flower year after year—for use only in borders and other permanent in-ground settings. But many of these versatile favorites are surprisingly effective as container plants, too. They have the obvious advantage of carryover from one year to the next. And enthusiastic gardeners enjoy the sequence of unfolding foliage, flower bloom, and even berries and fall foliage color that many perennials provide.

Perennials are the plants to choose as the basis of a more-or-less permanent container display—or at least one you can count on for several years. A perennial in a pot by itself can be brought to center stage when in full bloom, then moved to an out-of-the-way spot during its off-season (if its foliage is no asset) or combined with other pots of plants in bloom, perhaps as a foliage filler. Or you can plant a perennial in a larger pot with one or more companion plants, so that there are flower displays in succession—as you'd have in an in-ground flower border.

STAR PERFORMERS

The key to growing container perennials successfully is to select the right ones. In general, the best perennials for pots are those that flower over a long period or have good-looking foliage throughout the growing season. Also, choose plants that won't get too big. A dwarf or smaller-growing variety of a species may be the best choice.

To get even more mileage out of container perennials, look for plants that offer multiple advantages: interesting foliage texture or color, wonderful flowers, berries in fall, and so forth. (Of course, you can certainly choose a plant you can't resist even if it has just one special feature—a brief, showy bloom period, perhaps, or beautiful foliage.)

A great many perennials can be grown successfully in containers—just follow the basic selection guidelines and your own preferences. Of course, you'll need to keep in mind your climate and exposure conditions as well.

PLANTING TIPS

Don't *fill* a container with perennials; they'll soon grow and crowd the pot, and you'll have to repot. If one or two newly planted perennials look lonely in a pot, surround them with low-growing annuals that will fill in empty spaces with color while the perennials fill out.

As a general guide, an 18-inch-wide container will hold two 1-gallon plants, and a 20- to 24-inch-wide container will hold four or five 1-gallon plants.

CARING FOR PERENNIALS

Water perennials regularly and thoroughly during spring and summer growth periods, less frequently during the fall and winter dormant season. Apply a complete fertilizer monthly during the growing season.

For branching perennials that have a primary show of flowers, then another less profuse bloom period later, cut or shear back plants by one-half or more after the initial bloom period. This will encourage the best "second wave" of flowers. For branching perennials that have only one peak bloom period, cut back at the end of the growing season to encourage compactness and abundant bloom the following year. To keep perennials going from year to year, give them a "tune-up" when needed (see page 110).

Hosta

They're Not Weeds!

Admired for their fine textures, subtle colors, and graceful forms, ornamental grasses have come into their own as garden plants in recent years.

Many grasses are just too big for containers, but a stellar few are compact enough for pots. Combined with flowering perennials and annuals, they contribute a light, airy foliage effect to plant composition.

These grasses fall into two main categories: warm-season and cool-season. *Warm-season grasses* grow from spring through summer, often flower in fall, and then go dormant. These should be sheared back in spring, before new growth emerges. *Cool-season grasses* begin new growth in the fall, bloom in early spring (sometimes winter in mild climates), and are usually evergreen. Cut these back only when they look ragged—not necessarily every year. Divide all grasses every few years when they die back from the center; discard dead sections.

COOL-SEASON CONTAINER GRASSES:

Arrhenatherum elatius bulbosum 'Variegatum' (bulbous oat grass)
Carex (sedge), a grasslike perennial
Festuca ovina 'Glauca' (blue fescue)

WARM-SEASON CONTAINER GRASSES:

Miscanthus sinensis (maiden grass, eulalia grass),
   low-growing varieties
Pennisetum (fountain grass)
Stipa tenuissima (Mexican feather grass, Texas needle grass)

Lacy bouquet combines purple-leafed fountain grass and fox red curly sedge with delicately-textured perennials: yarrows, sedums, salvia, and purple loosestrife (an invasive plant that self-sows aggressively in summer-rainfall areas, outlawed in some states). Design: Orchard Nursery & Florist.

PERENNIAL FAVORITES

10 PERENNIALS FOR FLOWERS

Achillea (yarrow)
Agapanthus (lily-of-the-Nile)*
Aurinia saxatilis (basket-of-gold)
Chrysanthemum frutescens (marguerite)
Erigeron karvinskianus (Mexican daisy)
Gerbera jamesonii (Transvaal daisy)
Hemerocallis (daylily), shorter varieties*
Iberis sempervirens (evergreen candytuft)
Pelargonium (geranium)
Primula polyantha (polyanthus primrose)

10 PERENNIALS FOR FOLIAGE

Asparagus densiflorus 'Myers' (Myers asparagus)
Chlorophytum comosum (spider plant)
Dracaena marginata
Ferns, many varieties
Helichrysum petiolare (licorice plant)
Heuchera, several species and varieties
Hosta (plantain lily)
Lamium maculatum (dead nettle)
Liriope muscari (lily turf)
Phormium (New Zealand flax), shorter varieties

*Tuberous-rooted perennial, sometimes included among bulbs

A mass of tulips announces spring. OPPOSITE: Daffodils, tulips, and grape hyacinth share a half-barrel.

BULBS

A container blooming with sunny yellow tulips or sporting a single flame-hued clivia is a cheering sight on a deck or patio, in an entryway, or within a larger garden scheme. A pot of bulbs makes a stunning display by itself; tucking one in among other containers brings the whole group to life. And growing bulbs in containers lets you showcase your favorites for closer viewing than you might achieve with in-ground planting—then move them out of sight when blooms fade.

When you choose bulbs for containers, keep blooming season in mind. A carefully selected assortment with successive blooming periods will give you flowers from early spring right on into autumn—or even winter in some climates. As spring-blooming tulips fade, you can substitute a container of summer calla lilies; rotate pots again in autumn to display a dramatic canna.

Different bulbs have different life spans as container plants. Amaryllis and clivia, among others, are quite content to take up permanent residence in containers, producing splendid blooms year after year. But others—crocus, hyacinth, and iris, for example—usually provide just one glorious season of bloom in their containers. After that they need to be set out in the ground if you want them to bloom again.

The plants listed opposite include both true bulbs and other plants that sprout from similar structures—corms, rhizomes, tubers, and tuberous roots. Most go through a dormant period when their leaves wither and die back. Active growth resumes after dormancy, fueled by food stored in the bulb or bulblike structure.

PLANTING AND CARE

Choose plump, firm bulbs that feel heavy for their size. (Anemone and ranunculus are two exceptions—their tubers look dried and shrunken.) Plant bulbs soon after they appear for sale—in autumn for spring-flowering types, in late winter or early spring for summer and autumn bloomers. (For planting guidelines, see page 101.) For a massed "bouquet" effect, pack the container with Group 1 bulbs set close together, their sides almost touching. Dainty, low-growing bulbs like crocus or snowdrops are delightfully suited to wide, shallow containers, sometimes called bulb pans.

You don't need to fertilize bulbs that will spend only one season in a container. For bulbs that will stay in pots longer, use either water-soluble liquid fertilizer or timed-release fertilizer to keep them performing their best (see page 104). For the liquid fertilizer, make the first application when plants start to grow, then apply monthly during the growth and bloom period (or dilute to half strength and apply every other week). If you prefer timed-release fertilizer, scattering it on the soil at the start of the growing period may do it for spring- and summer-flowering bulbs that go dormant soon after flowering. For other bulbs, a second application after about 4 months is a good idea.

End-of-season care varies according to the types of bulbs you plant. Check the chart below, then consult page 109 to find out what you should do with each type of bulb after it has finished blooming.

FAVORITE CONTAINER BULBS

GROUP 1

Plant these in the ground after one bloom season in a pot.

Crocus
Hyacinthus (hyacinth)
Iris (bulbous types—Dutch, English,
    I. reticulata, I. danfordiae)
Muscari (grape hyacinth)
Narcissus (daffodil)
Tulipa (tulip)

GROUP 2

Grow these in pots for one bloom season, then dig out, store over winter, and repot next season (see page 109).

Achimenes
Begonia, tuberous kinds
Caladium bicolor
Dahlia, smaller kinds
Gloriosa rothschildiana (glory lily)
Polianthes tuberosa (tuberose)

GROUP 3

Leave these in the same pot for several to many years; repot when crowded. After the growth season, stop watering until growth resumes, usually the following year.

Canna
Clivia miniata (Kaffir lily)*
Convallaria majalis (lily-of-the-valley)
Cyclamen
Freesia
Hippeastrum (amaryllis)
Ixia (African corn lily)
Lilium (lily)*
Lycoris (spider lily)
Nerine
Ranunculus
Sparaxis tricolor (harlequin flower)
Tigridia pavonia (tiger flower)
Zantedeschia aethiopica (common calla)*
Zantedeschia, other species

*Water lightly when dormant.

CHILLING THOUGHTS

Some popular spring bulbs—notably tulips, hyacinths, and some crocus—need winter chill (temperatures lower than 40°F/4°C or so) to flower their best, on fully grown stems. The milder your climate, the more these bulbs (especially tulips) benefit from being chilled before you plant them.

Tulip and hyacinth bulbs

In warm-winter areas such as Southern California, the Gulf Coast, and the low desert of the Southwest, bulbs definitely benefit from a chilling session. Where winters are mild but still frosty, bulbs should get cold enough sitting outdoors in their pots through the winter.

To chill bulbs, place them in a mesh bag or a paper bag with holes punched to allow air circulation (bulbs stored in plastic bags may rot). Refrigerate at 40° to 45°F/4° to 7°C for at least 4 to 6 weeks. Store away from fruit like apples, which give off ethylene gas that can damage developing buds.

To grow spring container bulbs in extreme-cold climates, plant in plastic pots in the fall, water, and sink in a foot-deep trench. Cover with mulch and plastic until temperatures consistently stay in the teens or above.

Zantedeschia aethiopica

Double-flowered 'Crown of Bohemia' and single 'Brilliant' hibiscus bloom in 15-inch pots.

Many evergreen shrubs can serve these design functions all year round in mild-winter climates. Deciduous shrubs (the ones that drop their leaves in winter) provide foliage and flowers in spring and summer, and sometimes stunning leaf color in autumn.

The best container shrubs are compact, slow-growing varieties. Many shrubs have dwarf counterparts (often with "*nana*" in their botanical names) that are well suited for containers.

Keep your climate in mind. If you live in a mild-winter area, almost any of the shrubs listed at right will work for you. If you live where winters are freezing, you'll have to protect containers; tender shrubs will require moving indoors—a big job because they may be very heavy and bulky.

PLANTING AND CARE

You can plant shrubs at almost any time of year, but spring is preferable in cold-winter areas, early autumn to mid-winter in mild-winter regions. Many shrubs do best in standard lightweight potting soil mix; others tolerate a heavier mixture of half garden loam, half potting mix. Some, such as camellias and rhododendrons, need a special acid potting mix. Ask at the nursery about the shrubs you choose, or consult a garden guide.

Plant a new shrub in a container that's a few inches bigger all around than its nursery can or pot. Most shrubs will eventually need larger pots, but the sizing-up should be done gradually.

In general, shrubs appreciate a monthly application of a complete fertilizer throughout their growing season (spring through summer). If you plant in spring or summer, wait two weeks before the first application. Don't fertilize autumn and winter-planted shrubs until spring.

Aucuba japonica

SHRUBS

Showcasing a shrub in a container—perhaps a glossy-leafed holly, a heavenly bamboo tinged with red, or a lavishly-flowered hibiscus—lets you appreciate its best qualities at close range. Many shrubs have striking shapes, dramatic foliage, or colorful flowers; in containers, they become handsome centerpieces in your garden design. Even "ordinary" shrubs such as oleander or lantana can be eye-catching solo performers in the right container.

You can plant a shrub in a pot by itself as a focal point or use one as the centerpiece of a mixed container planting that includes annuals or other filler plants. You can also use rows or groupings of container shrubs to create a low screen or define a seating area. And shrubs can be the backbone of an all-in-pots garden on a rooftop or deck.

STANDARD TIME

A "tree" from a bush? It's standard operating procedure. You can transform a shrub or vine that's normally bushy all over into a "standard"—a simulated tree with single, upright trunk and a bushy topknot.

Choose a plant with a single main stem (see suggestions at right) and remove side shoots up to 3½ feet above base. Your shrub or vine may need to be staked for support, at least in the early stages; tie it to the stake in several places. Turn the plant regularly to keep it from leaning toward the sun.

When the plant reaches the desired height, you may want to trim the crown into a rounded ball, the style that gives standards the nickname "lollipop trees." If your standard is a vine, let its stems cascade down naturally.

To keep your standard from reverting to shrub form, remove any suckers that emerge along the trunk. Continue to prune and trim to control growth of the head.

SOME STANDARD FAVORITES

Bottlebrush	India hawthorn
(Callistemon)	*(Rhaphiolepis indica)*
Bougainvillea	Lantana
Camellia	Princess flower
Euryops	*(Tibouchina urvilleana)*
Flowering maple	Rose
(Abutilon hybridum)	Rosemary
Fuchsia	Southern Indica azalea
Hibiscus	

Standard-trained *Abutilon* is underplanted with yellow crotons and yellow and orange Hiemalis begonias.

FAVORITE CONTAINER SHRUBS

12 DECIDUOUS SHRUBS

Berberis thunbergii (Japanese barberry)
Buddleia davidii (butterfly bush, summer lilac)
Caryopteris clandonensis (bluebeard, blue mist)
Deutzia gracilis (slender deutzia)
Fuchsia
Hydrangea macrophylla (bigleaf hydrangea)
Lagerstroemia indica (crape myrtle), shrubby ones
Paeonia (tree peony)
Potentilla fruticosa (cinquefoil)
Punica granatum (pomegranate)
Rhododendron (deciduous azaleas)
Weigela florida 'Variegata'

14 EVERGREEN SHRUBS

Abutilon hybridum (flowering maple)
Aucuba japonica (Japanese aucuba)
Brugmansia (angel's trumpet)
Buxus (boxwood)
Camellia
Fatsia japonica (Japanese aralia)
Gardenia jasminoides

Hibiscus rosa-sinensis (Chinese or tropical hibiscus)
Ilex (holly)
Lantana
Mahonia, many varieties
Nandina domestica (heavenly bamboo)
Nerium oleander (oleander)
Rhododendron (azalea, rhododendron)

5 SHRUBBY CONIFERS

Juniperus, many varieties
Picea glauca 'Conica' (dwarf Alberta spruce)
Pinus mugo mugo (mugho pine)
Sciadopitys verticillata (umbrella pine)
Taxus baccata (English yew)

ROSE IS A ROSE IS A ROSE...IN A POT

Opinions vary as to just what Gertrude Stein meant with her circuitous line of poetry. What most people do recognize is the rose's claim to enthronement as queen of flowers. Long a staple in the garden, roses are increasingly available in varieties suitable for container gardening, too.

The best roses for containers have smallish leaves and flowers, as well as a compact growth habit. The following are eight varieties that adapt well to pots; each is available in both standard and bush form.

'BONICA'. Easy-to-grow, lightly scented pink shrub.

'CUPCAKE'. One of the best pink miniatures.

'GOURMET POPCORN'. White, shrubby miniature with cascading habit, constant bloom.

'HEARTBREAKER'. Rounded cream-and-pink miniature with dark, glossy leaves.

'LITTLE ARTIST'. Fragrant red-and-yellow miniature with glossy leaves.

'MAGIC CARROUSEL'. White miniature edged in red.

'SWEET CHARIOT'. Fragrant purple miniature, slightly cascading.

'THE FAIRY'. Rounded pink shrub.

Roses are available both in nursery cans and bare-root. Look for plants with three or more strong, well-spaced canes that are green and hard. On bare-root plants, roots should be well-developed, unknotted, and unbroken.

PLANTING YOUR ROSE

While miniature roses can do well in pots as small as 2-gallon nursery cans, regular-size bushes, standards, and climbers need lots of root room. A 24-inch pot is a good size for a shrub or floribunda, an 18-inch pot for a miniature tree.

Use a well-draining, non-compacting potting medium —either a packaged potting mix or your own mixture of organic material (for porosity) and garden soil (to hold in nutrients and moisture).

For a rose in a nursery can, follow the directions on page 101 for gallon and larger pots. For a bare-root rose, plant as described for bare-root plants, setting the rose on top of the soil mound so that the bud union (or the brown area above roots on non-budded miniatures) is just below the pot rim. Spread roots over the mound, trimming to fit the container if necessary, and proceed according to the basic planting guidelines.

CARING FOR A ROSE

For the happiest rose, position it where the container is shaded (for cool roots) but the plant itself isn't. Light shade during afternoon heat is good for both plant and container.

Water often enough so that soil stays moist but not soggy. Feed with a dilute liquid fertilizer every other week or so *or* use a controlled-release fertilizer 3 or 4 times during the growing season.

After a few years, when the rose is dormant in winter, tap the rootball out of the pot, rub the soil away, and trim long or coiled roots. Prune out dead or crossing branches. Then repot in fresh potting soil.

'Bonica' rose

CACTI AND SUCCULENTS

Fascinating, often showy and dramatic, cacti and succulents are a perfect match for containers. They're unfussy, easy-to-grow plants, most of which thrive in full sun. And though they need periodic watering, most need it less frequently than other container plants—after all, many of these are the plants that create desert landscapes.

With rare exceptions, every cactus is a succulent, a plant that stores water in its tissues. But not every succulent is a cactus. Cacti are distinguished from other succulents by their *areoles*— well-defined areas on the plant surface from which sprout spines, bristles, or hairs, and also flowers. Choose smaller kinds of cacti and almost any succulent to grow in containers.

PLANTING TIPS

You can plant cacti and succulents in almost any kind of pot; just be careful not to overwater, especially if you use plastic or other non-porous pots. For round cactus plants, choose a container at least 2 inches wider than the plant; for more vertical plants, use a container as wide as half the plant's height to create visual balance. Small cacti and succulents also make delightful dish gardens.

You can buy a special soil mix for cacti and succulents or mix your own, using one part peat-moss–based soil mix (such as packaged house plant mix) and two parts builder's sand or fine gravel to provide the good drainage these plants need.

When planting a spiny cactus, protect your hands by wearing thick gloves and lifting the plant with a thick strap fashioned from folded newspaper. You can also use kitchen tongs to lift small cacti.

ONGOING CARE

For most cacti and succulents, you should place containers where they'll get full sun. It's best to water these plants fairly regularly during their active spring-to-summer growth period. Soak the soil thoroughly, then wait until it's almost completely dry before watering again. Fertilize monthly during that period with ¼-strength complete liquid fertilizer. Cut back to about one watering a month and stop fertilizing during the autumn-winter rest period.

In very mild climates, these plants can live outdoors all year. In cold-winter areas, bring them indoors as house plants, placing them where they'll get plenty of light.

Most cacti and succulents need repotting every 2 to 3 years; do this in early spring.

Barrel cactus in a footed clay pot is backed by prickly pear.

CONTAINER FAVORITES

Many species in each of the following cacti and succulent genera make fine container plants.

12 CACTI

Chamaecereus sylvestri (peanut cactus)	*Lobivia*
Cleistocactus	*Lobivopsis*
Coryphantha	*Mammillaria*
Echinocactus (barrel cactus)	*Notocactus*
Echinopsis (Easter lily cactus, sea urchin cactus)	*Opuntia*
	Parodia
	Rebutia

12 SUCCULENTS

Aeonium	*Gasteria*
Agave	*Haworthia*
Aloe	*Kalanchoe*
Crassula (jade plant, others)	*Sedum* (stonecrop)
Dudleya	*Sempervivum* (houseleek, hen and chickens)
Echeveria (hen and chicks, others)	
Euphorbia	

VINES

Their happy habit of rambling along fence tops and climbing up trellised walls makes vines a delightful addition to any garden. A vine grown in a container can play many useful roles—as a portable garden screen (with a trellis attached to the container), as a backdrop for other container plants, or spilling over the edges of a container to soften the lines of an arrangement. Vines can provide lush green foliage, brilliant flowers, and even arresting autumn leaf color.

To ensure well-behaved vines that won't get out of hand, it's important to select kinds that are appropriate for containers and to keep them carefully trained and pruned. Avoid very fast-growing vines such as honeysuckle and trumpet vine.

You'll find it easiest to get container vines started from 1- to 2-year-old vines in gallon containers. The exceptions are annuals such as morning glories and scarlet runner beans, which you'll need to start from seeds.

Some vines, such as cup-and-saucer vine and clematis, have attaching devices: tiny sucker discs, rootlets, tendrils, or twining stems. These plants cling easily by themselves to nearly any support you provide—trellis, post, or wire. Those with rootlets (like ivy) or sucker discs can even cling to walls and fences. Other vines, such as bougainvillea and star jasmine, need a little help; to train these, tie them to the support with raffia, soft twine, or soft plastic plant ties.

CARING FOR VINES

During the growing season, all vines should be guided along their supports, or tied on. Train new growth diligently; pinch back if needed to keep plants looking lush and tidy. Give vigorous growers such as bougainvillea or passion vine a thorough pruning in early spring, before new growth starts. Fertilize vines monthly from spring through summer with a complete fertilizer.

Thunbergia alata

If you want to grow tender vines where winter temperatures dip below freezing, you must be able to move the plants in their containers to a sheltered place; this may mean cutting them off their supports (if they're not fastened to the container) and pruning them back.

It's a snap to grow annual vines; just guide their stems up a trellis or other support when necessary.

Bougainvillea

MADE FOR CLIMBING

A vine-adorned trellis can serve as a sculptural focal point in your garden, screen unwanted features from view, or create a sense of privacy for a deck or patio. You'll find ready-made trellises available in catalogs, nurseries, and garden centers in many styles and price ranges. They might be hand-crafted or mass-produced, made of hand-forged metal, wire, woven vines, or wood.

Most trellises are simple to use and come ready to install. Choose a small one to fit your container, then either push the feet into the soil (before planting, to avoid damaging roots) or attach them to the outside of the container. You can use a larger trellis if you mount it on a wall or fence directly behind the container in which the vine is planted.

The assortment of trellis designs shown here gives an idea of the range of decorative styles available for use in containers.

Architectural cupola trellis provides charming support for a vine.

VINES FOR CONTAINERS

6 ANNUAL VINES

Bean, scarlet runner
Cobaea scandens (cup-and-saucer vine)*
Ipomoea nil, quamoclit, tricolor
    (morning glory, cypress vine,
    cardinal climber)
Lathyrus odoratus (sweet pea)
Thunbergia alata
    (black-eyed Susan vine)*
Tropaeolum majus, peregrinum
    (nasturtium, canary bird flower)

*Tender perennial usually grown as annual

12 WOODY VINES

Bougainvillea
Clematis, especially hybrids
Clerodendrum thomsoniae
    (bleeding heart glorybower)
Fatshedera lizei
Gelsemium sempervirens
    (Carolina jessamine)
Hardenbergia
Hedera helix (English ivy)
Lonicera (honeysuckle), some
Mandevilla

Parthenocissus (Virginia creeper,
    Boston ivy, others)
Passiflora (passion vine)
Trachelospermum jasminoides
    (star jasmine)

Passiflora alatocaerulea

A Japanese maple *(Acer palmatum)* in a pot becomes the focal point of this patio.

TREES

A handsome small tree can add a welcome element of structure to your container garden. Container-cultivated trees—modest in height, yet still tall enough to look dramatic—can enhance even the smallest balcony, patio, or entryway. They can act as focal points in their own right or as backdrops and vertical accents with flowering plants.

The best trees for containers are small in scale and tidy in habit. Avoid trees that litter—that drop lots of leaves, berries, or fruits throughout the growing season. Choose trees, like those listed on the facing page, with relatively well-behaved root systems. Smaller varieties of many trees are also available that will give you a shrubbier form than the plants listed opposite.

For information about fruit trees, see page 52. To find out about keeping a Christmas tree in a pot, turn to page 93.

CARING FOR TREES

With proper care, most slow-growing small trees will prosper in containers for years. Just make sure you choose a container with sufficient room for root growth (and for staking a young tree, if

that's a temporary necessity); 18 inches across should be considered the bare minimum.

You'll need to trim roots and repot as the tree grows (see page 111) or move up to a larger pot. And at some point your tree may need to be planted in the ground in order to thrive.

You can plant trees whenever you choose, but early autumn to mid-winter is best in mild-winter climates, spring in cold-winter areas. (Bare-root trees usually appear in nurseries in mid-winter to early spring, depending on the climate in your area.) Apply a complete fertilizer once in spring, once again in summer.

In mild climates, many trees can live outdoors year-round. But in cold-winter areas you must consider how you'll overwinter a tree in a pot (see pages 106–107).

CREATING AN ESPALIER

A container tree or shrub can take on a whole new style when it's espaliered rather than pruned into a conventional shape. Devised in Europe during the 16th and 17th centuries as an ingenious space-saving method of raising fruit trees, espalier is often used nowadays for purely decorative purposes as well.

Trees, shrubs, and even vines can be espaliered. Just be sure the branches are flexible enough to train. Even deciduous plants add interest to the garden year-round when they're espaliered. After the last fruit has been picked and the last leaf has fallen, the bare branches create a bold, sculptural pattern.

An espalier is trained to grow flat, spreading out along a trellis attached to the plant's container. You can train a formal, symmetrical espalier in a traditional pattern, or choose a more freeform design. The basic idea is to direct branches in a two-dimensional pattern, pruning away any branches that obscure the pattern. Don't expect the full design to become clear immediately; it may take several years of diligent training. Fruit trees in particular require

careful attention; when pruning, be sure not to snip off fruiting buds or spurs.

If you are creating a formal espalier pattern, bend the branches you want to grow horizontally down at a 45° angle at the start of the growing season, securing them to the trellis with soft plastic nursery ties. Gradually lower and retie branches as the season progresses so that they are horizontal by the end of the season. Then you can train one branch vertically, depending on your chosen pattern, and remove other shoots. Add new horizontal tiers to the design in successive growth seasons by tying and pruning branches as necessary.

For an informal design, just follow the plant's natural shape, using your own sense of artistry as a guide.

Candelabra pattern   Palmette pattern   Double U-shape pattern

CONTAINER TREE CHOICES

10 EVERGREEN TREES

Abies nordmanniana (Nordmann fir)

Araucaria heterophylla
(Norfolk Island pine)

Arbutus unedo (strawberry tree)

Callistemon citrinus (lemon bottlebrush)

Laurus nobilis (sweet bay)

Palms, smaller varieties
(such as *Phoenix roebelenii*)

Pinus densiflora 'Umbraculifera'
(Tanyosho pine)

Pinus thunbergiana
(Japanese black pine)

Podocarpus

Pyrus kawakamii (evergreen pear)

10 DECIDUOUS TREES

Acer palmatum (Japanese maple)

Amelanchier grandiflora

Cercis canadensis
(Eastern redbud)

Chionanthus virginicus

Halesia carolina

Magnolia loebneri

Magnolia soulangiana

Prunus (flowering cherry,
flowering plum)

Stewartia monadelpha

Styrax

Laurus nobilis
'Saratoga'

Dwarf apple tree grows as an informal espalier.

FRUIT TREES FOR CONTAINERS

Many favorite as well as unusual citrus trees are available in dwarf forms; these are the best for containers.

Dwarf apple, apricot, nectarine, peach, pear, plum

Dwarf citrus: kumquat, lemon, mandarin orange, orange, lime, calamondin (mandarin-kumquat hybrid)

Fig (edible-fruit kinds)

Loquat (*Eriobotrya japonica*)

Pineapple guava (*Feijoa sellowiana*)*

Strawberry guava (*Psidium cattleianum*)*

*Fruiting shrubs rather than trees

FRUIT TREES

Though not every kind of fruit tree can be grown successfully in a container, many—especially dwarf varieties—do very well if given adequate room for their roots and proper care. Dwarf fruit trees bear full-size fruit despite their modest height.

The attractive foliage, form, and flowers of many fruit trees are welcome additions to any garden. To emphasize the decorative aspects of these trees in containers, you can train their branches into a flat pattern as espaliers—see page 51. Or you can underplant a fruit tree with attractive low-growing plants.

PLANTING AND CARE

Choose a large planter box or half barrel that allows plenty of room for roots—ideally one that holds at least 2 cubic feet of soil, but at a bare minimum 18 inches across. You can find nursery trees in cans or (in winter or early spring) in bare-root form. Depending on your climate, winter to early spring is the best time to plant either.

For the most abundant fruit crop, take care to give your plants sufficient water and fertilizer. Never let the soil dry out completely. Fertilize once a month from spring through summer, using a complete fertilizer for fruit trees or a special citrus fertilizer for citrus. Note that most trees need at least 6 hours of sunshine a day.

Consider your tree's requirements for overwintering (see pages 106–107). If your area experiences hard freezes, you can grow citrus quite successfully as an indoor-outdoor plant. Before the first frost, move the tree to a well-lighted basement, garage, or unheated room of the house (citrus needs plenty of light or it will drop all its leaves). Water enough to keep the soil from completely drying out but not enough so that it stays saturated; don't fertilize. Return the plant to the outdoors after danger of frost has passed.

Calamondin

PORTABLE TOPIARIES

Charm and grace—those are two words that come readily to mind when viewing these small-scale topiaries. They are miniature versions of the topiaries you might envision gracing a country estate, where shrubs and even trees might be pruned and trained into formal shapes to resemble geometric figures or fantasy animals.

It's surprisingly easy to make portable versions of topiaries to serve as elegant porch or patio accents, and even to come indoors for brief appearances. You just train vining plants around wire frames that you can buy in classical or whimsical shapes. Or you can make a simple frame yourself by bending wire coat hangers into a wreath or heart shape.

Painted or coated frames are good for outdoor use, since they're less likely to rust. A general guideline for size: when the frame is inserted into the container, the part of the frame exposed should be about 2 or 3 times the height of the container. Simple shapes are easiest to work with.

Select a heavy container (such as a terra-cotta planter) at least 8 to 12 inches across to provide a stable base. Then follow these steps to create an elegant patio accent.

Insert the wire frame into the pot, securing it with potting soil.

Plant a vining plant (suggestions follow) at the base of the frame.

Wrap 2 or 3 plant runners, one at a time, around a wire. Wrap in both directions. If runners are stiff, tie them to the frame with cotton string or plastic plant ties until they have grown in place.

Repeat wrapping for each wire.

As runners grow, continue training them around the frame. Maintain the shape you want by clipping or pinching new growth as necessary. Water regularly, and feed once in the spring with a complete fertilizer.

Your plant should thrive in its container for 3 years or so; then you'll need to give it more room.

PLANTS TO TRAIN

Many vining plants work for wire-frame topiary, but the smaller the frame you choose, the smaller the leaf size should be or the frame shape will be obscured. Ivies with leaves about an inch across work well. These are some good choices:

- Bougainvillea
- Jasmine (*Jasminum polyanthum*)
- Mandevilla
- Rosemary
- Small-leafed ivies, such as *Hedera helix* (English ivy)

Buy young plants with pliable stems. A 6-inch pot of ivy with plenty of runners is enough to start a small topiary.

English ivy forms a wreath around a poinsettia plant in its own tiny pot; when seasons change, another plant can be set in place at the base of the topiary.

Growing green beans and other vegetables in hanging pots helps protect tender plants from garden pests and brings produce into easy reach for harvesting.

VEGETABLES

Do you have visions of growing your own plump red tomatoes, crisp peppers, and crunchy carrots but feel thwarted by lack of space for a garden plot, or by the fact that all the sun in your yard falls on your brick patio? With containers, you can overcome problems of poor soil, heavy root competition, or shade. And vegetables in containers can be a handsome addition to a patio or deck, especially when grouped with a few pots of flowering plants.

Many new varieties of high-yield dwarf vegetables for containers have been developed in recent years; compact tomatoes are especially successful. But you may find that standard-size plants (excluding real ramblers like potatoes and winter squash) are more productive and yield tastier vegetables. Just be sure to plant them in generous-sized containers. Avoid "whopper" tomatoes—choose standard or cherry-size ones instead.

Certain vegetables or vegetable varieties perform best in particular climates; ask nursery personnel for guidance.

Although you can certainly start vegetables from seed, you'll get quicker results with some kinds if you begin with nursery transplants. Root vegetables, however, are usually best to start from seed—it can be tricky to transplant taprooted plants. Soil warms more quickly in the spring in containers than it does in the ground, so container vegetables get a fast start and produce early.

PLANTING

Shallow-rooted crops such as chard, green onions, radishes, and spinach are easy to grow in almost any container. Carrots, beets, and other root crops—and even potatoes—will work as long as the container is deep enough. For carrots, choose a container twice as deep as the length the carrots will reach at maturity.

To get a good harvest from vegetables with extensive root systems—such as cucumbers, potatoes, summer squash, and tomatoes—use containers at least 16 inches deep and 20 inches wide. Broccoli, eggplant, and peppers can get by with slightly smaller pots, 12 to 14 inches deep and slightly wider.

When to plant depends on what you're planting. While some vegetables grow best in cool soil and can live

Tomato

POTATOES IN A POT

Here's an easy technique for planting potatoes in a container. Plant from seed potatoes (cut into 2-inch chunks, each with at least one eye) in a large, deep pot filled halfway with potting soil. When the potato plants reach the top of the pot, add more soil to fill the container almost all the way up.

Look for seed potatoes at a nursery or feed store, or in a catalog.

Just tip the pot to harvest.

FAVORITE CONTAINER VEGETABLES

WARM-SEASON VEGETABLES

Beans

Cucumbers

Eggplant

Peppers

Summer squashes

Tomatoes

COOL-SEASON VEGETABLES

Beets

Broccoli

Cabbage, some

Carrots

Green onions/scallions

Kale, some

Peas

Radishes

Spinach

through a light frost, others need warm to hot weather and won't survive frost. Plant *cool-season vegetables* (such as broccoli and radishes) in early spring, several weeks *before* the average last spring frost date for your locale; if you live in a mild climate, you can plant again in fall for a winter harvest. *Warm-season vegetables* (such as beans and tomatoes) should be planted only *after* the danger of frost is over in spring.

Vegetables do fine in a standard potting mix, with controlled-release fertilizer worked in at planting time. Place containers where plants will get full sun for at least 6 hours a day.

CARE AND HARVESTING

Annual vegetables need a constant supply of water and nutrients. Never let the soil dry out or plants will wilt. To supplement timed-release fertilizer in the potting mix, feed every 2 to 3 weeks with a half-strength liquid fertilizer solution.

For highest yields and a tidy appearance, vining crops like cucumbers, tomatoes, and beans should be staked or trained on wire supports, or caged in wire frames.

In cold-winter climates, protect tender plants from unseasonable late frosts in spring by one of the methods described on page 107. In extremely hot areas, put containers where they'll get afternoon shade.

BERRIES BY THE BARREL

Strawberries are the easiest berries to grow in containers. They will flourish in a half-barrel, tub, or, of course, the ever-popular strawberry jar—the classic pocket planter. Select a disease-resistant variety; check with a local nursery to find one suitable for your area.

Set out about a dozen plants if you're planting in a barrel; to plant in a pocket planter, insert one plant per pocket and a couple at the top (see page 75). Plant in early spring, in standard potting soil, with the container placed where berries will get at least 6 hours of full sun daily.

To make the plant stronger, pinch off the first flowers. Water regularly so that soil stays moist, but don't overwater or the fruit will taste weak. Fertilize when growth begins and again after the first crop; overfertilizing will reduce fruit sweetness. Plants usually bear a small harvest the first year, more in years to follow.

Strawberries need protection where winters are severe and where alternate freezing and thawing are common. When soil freezes, cover plants with straw several inches deep, or move to a garage or basement.

SALAD IN A POT

GREAT CONTAINER GREENS

Arugula

Curly cress

Endive

Escarole

Leaf lettuce, many varieties

Mizuna

Mustard

Radicchio

Sorrel (perennial)

SALAD FLOWERS

Add flair to your salads by growing some of these edible blossoms to toss with greens:

Calendula

Johnny jump-up

Nasturtium

Pansy

Violet

Pansies

Leafy and luscious, salad greens are among the easiest and most rewarding edibles you can grow in containers. Set out a pot-full of greens in a mild, sunny spot just outside your door and you'll be able to step out and pluck fresh greens for your dinner salad just minutes before you're ready to eat. Lettuce and other greens are so adaptable, you can grow them in just about anything—a window box, a bowl-shaped pot, even a hanging basket.

Seedlings of many gourmet leaf lettuces and other salad greens are available in many nurseries. Nurseries and seed catalogs also offer many of the less common types of lettuce in seed form.

In very mild-winter areas, you can plant these cool-season edibles in winter; wait until spring elsewhere. Buy an assortment; experimenting with various types is fun, and they reach harvest size so quickly that you can soon replace them with other varieties if you wish. For added color, tuck in an edible flower, too.

PLANTING AND CARE

Plant in a fairly wide container (at least 14 inches) of average depth. Greens benefit from a rich soil mix—see page 99. Mix in a timed-release fertilizer at planting time.

Plant as for any annual, arranging tall greens (like mustard) in the center of the container. You can crowd plants in (3 or 4 inches apart), since you'll be harvesting regularly. Or you can start lettuce from seed—see page 36.

Keep the soil evenly moist, and fertilize every 2 weeks using a liquid fertilizer at half strength to promote continued leaf growth. Cut off outer leaves when they're young and tender. The key to a plentiful salad supply is to continuously cut bite-size leaves; just drop them directly into your salad spinner to wash, and they're ready to serve.

To keep pots going all season, pull out mature plants after 4 or 5 cuttings and replace with new ones.

CULINARY HERBS

Herbs are an almost indispensable addition to any cook's garden. As attractive to look at as they are tasty and aromatic, fresh herbs add a special touch to salads, soups, and other dishes. Keep a pot of mixed herbs on your deck, back porch, or windowsill, with a pair of scissors hanging close at hand, and you can easily snip basil leaves to toss with pasta or rosemary sprigs to flavor a roasting chicken.

The added appeal for container gardeners is the fact that herbs are so unfussy; in fact, some actually thrive in fairly dry conditions. And containers are a good way to keep rapid spreaders like mint from taking over the garden.

Some herbs, like basil and cilantro, are annuals; others, like oregano and sage, are perennials that live from year to year.

PLANTING AND CARE

You can grow herbs in almost any container—a window box, a good-sized planter bowl, or even a strawberry pot. Some herbs will grow well in quite small pots, but they'll need more frequent watering. All herbs thrive in sun, although a few (such as basil and mint) also tolerate partial shade.

You can start many herbs from seed, but planting from 2-inch nursery pots or cell-packs gives you satisfyingly quick results. Plant in spring, in a standard potting mix.

Fertilize herbs with a half-strength liquid solution once a month through spring and summer; water regularly.

You can begin harvesting as soon as a good number of leaves appear on young plants. Snip off leaves as you need them, but avoid trimming off more than a third of the foliage at a time. Constant trimming for cooking keeps plants bushy and producing plenty of new growth.

If you live in a cold-winter area, give perennial herbs some shelter when temperatures are expected to get down to 20°F/−7°C (see page 106). If the temperature consistently drops to 10°F/−12°C or lower, bring them indoors to a well-lighted garage or unheated room of the house.

In early spring, cut back tired-looking perennial herbs and add new annuals; begin fertilizing again. Replant annual herbs as necessary to replenish your supply during the growing season.

Mint

FAVORITE CONTAINER HERBS

Basil	Mint
Chervil	Oregano
Chives	Parsley
Cilantro (Chinese parsley, coriander)	Rosemary
	Sage
Dill	Tarragon
Marjoram	Thyme

Wagonful of herbs includes silver thyme, chives, and borage.

A HOME FOR FISH

An 18-inch-diameter container can accommodate about four fish. To make your fish feel at home before releasing them, place them—still in their plastic bag—in the water garden for about 20 minutes. Make sure the water will not be too hot for the fish.

Don't overfeed your fish—you could disturb the ecological balance in your pond. In cold climates, move fish to an indoor aquarium during the winter.

A WATER GARDEN IN A TUB

It's been said that a garden without water is like a theater without a stage. Of course, that means ponds and pools and fountains, not hoses and drip systems. A pondlike tub filled with water-loving plants can form a cool oasis on even a small deck or patio.

Properly placed, a container water garden can reflect the blue of the sky and the colors of nearby plants. And don't be surprised if your aquatic garden doubles as a birdbath. Especially during hot spells, birds may visit to drink and preen among the leaves.

To introduce water-garden refreshment into a container collection, you'll need a leakproof container, water plants in plastic pots, and a few goldfish or mosquito fish to keep the water free of insects.

Almost any large container will work, but to house a standard water lily or lotus you'll probably need one at least 18 inches across; a 25-gallon container is a good size. If the container you choose isn't waterproof, you'll need to line it with a flexible pond liner (PVC or EPDM), pleated to fit. Or you could hide a watertight tub inside the more attractive "show" container you've selected.

You don't have to limit yourself to commercially available tubs for water gardens. You might consider using a ceramic urn or a wooden half-barrel (scrubbed and lined)—or a cast-iron soup kettle, a terra-cotta pot, a metal watering trough, or a sturdy plastic tub (some look like terra-cotta).

CHOOSING WATER PLANTS

How many plants you can use depends on the size of your container. One water lily per square yard of surface area is plenty, along with a few bunches of oxygenating plants or grasses. For smaller containers, try dwarf water lilies or grasses.

Don't crowd too many plants into your water garden. Let the water show, too. A combination of opposites—small and large plants, tall and short ones—can be the most pleasing to the eye.

When you buy your plants, ask about their requirements for overwintering in your climate zone.

Tub garden on deck features big arrow-shaped leaves of *Xanthosoma sagittifolium,* shorter *Xanthosoma violaceum,* and grasslike *Carex morrowii* 'Variegata' and *Phalaris arundinacea.*

HOW TO PROCEED

Position your container where it will get at least 6 hours of sun daily. A water-filled 25-gallon container weighs more than 200 pounds—make sure your chosen spot can bear its concentrated weight. Then follow these steps:

1 Fill container about two-thirds full with water.

2 Position your plants, in their pots, in the water so that pot tops will be 6 inches or more under water. (Adding an inch of sand in the top of your pots will help keep the soil from floating out.) Some plants do best if only partly submerged—set pots on bricks or upturned pots. Free-floating plants don't need to be potted. (Ask about your plants when you buy them.)

3 Fill the tub the rest of the way with water.

4 Add goldfish or mosquito fish.

TUB MAINTENANCE

Keep the water level topped, remove floating debris, and cut off dead leaves on an ongoing basis. About once a year, drain the container and scrub it out with a solution of 4 parts water to 1 part bleach. Rinse well.

Chinese water bowls hold arrowhead, dwarf bullrush, and water iris.

POPULAR WATER PLANTS

Arrowhead *(Sagittaria latifolia).* White flower spikes, arching leaves; submerge pot.

Dwarf papyrus *(Cyperus isocladus).* Long, narrow leaves and flowers; submerge pot.

Horsetail *(Equisetum hyemale).* Rushlike, jointed hollow stems; submerge pot halfway.

Japanese iris *(Iris ensata).* Velvety blooms, sword-shaped leaves; submerge pot halfway. Remove pot from water during plant's dormant season.

Lotus *(Nelumbo).* Showy flowers, big round leaves above water; submerge pot.

Umbrella plant *(Cyperus alternifolius).* Spreading leaves; submerge pot.

Water hyacinth *(Eichhornia crassipes).* Violet flowers, floating leaves; free-floating. (Don't turn loose in natural bodies of water.)

Water lily *(Nymphaea).* Showy flowers, round floating leaves; submerge pot.

Glazed Chinese urn makes a dramatic pond for water lilies.

A wooden tub sporting a tumble of sun-drenched nasturtiums, blanket flowers, and marigolds . . . a cool composition of green ferns, silvery dusty miller, and white impatiens . . . or

GREAT CONTAINER
DESIGNS

a hanging basket spilling over with skeins of ivy and lobelia—these are a few of the delightful effects you can achieve with a mixed container planting. Such arrangements may look spontaneous, but a really stunning container design is usually the result of careful planning. When you're combining plants in a pot, even a little forethought goes a long way.

In this chapter, you'll find practical advice that takes the mystery out of designing with plants. You'll learn about principles of shape and structure, use of color and texture, and style considerations. You'll also learn by example as you browse through a gallery of container "recipes." The ingredients needed for these designs, along with sun and water requirements, appear alongside photos of each container.

You may want to recreate these arrangements just as they are shown, or you may feel like experimenting, substituting one plant for another or adapting the color scheme to your own garden plan. Or you may want to strike out in entirely new directions, following the general design principles in this chapter to come up with your own unique creations.

A mixed bouquet of marigolds, coreopsis, petunias, and caladium makes a charming composition when planted in a rustic basket. Design: Walter and Fran Bull.

PUTTING IT ALL TOGETHER

When it comes to assembling and combining plants and matching them with your containers, let your own tastes and instincts be your principal guides. You'll naturally gravitate toward colors, styles, and forms that please you, so that whatever you create will bear your personal stamp. Part of the fun of container gardening is the chance it gives you to experiment—to be playful and to try out plants and plant combinations on a temporary basis. In the relatively limited environment of a container, you can plant, rearrange, rotate, and discard plantings more freely than you might be willing to try with plants in the ground. Just be sure that the plants you choose to share a container all have similar requirements for soil, water, and sun.

SHAPE AND STRUCTURE

Together, a container and the plants it holds have an overall shape or structure in somewhat the same way a floral arrangement does. A very casual design, such as a friendly mix of annuals in a standard-shaped flowerpot, may have a loose, informal structure. Another arrangement may have a stronger, more deliberate element of form. A design may be tall and dramatic or low and rounded. It may be fan-shaped or triangular, horizontal, or even asymmetrical. Keeping in mind the structural form you are creating may help you when it comes to positioning plants in your container.

Consider plant forms and how they'll contribute to the overall design structure. "Form" refers to a plant's shape and growth habit—vining or upright-growing, pyramidal, rounded, vase-shaped, spreading, spiky, or irregular. Although you may be able to prune and train many plants to direct the shape they take, in a container it's best to choose plants that will naturally give you the shape you want. Be sure to take into account the form the plant will have when it grows in.

It's generally helpful to think of plants as playing one of three basic design roles in an arrangement: as *vertical accents*; as *fillers*, for bulk and color; or as *cascaders* to spill over a container's edges and soften the look of the design. (A plant may fit into more than one category, depending on its age and size, and on what other plants are being used in an arrangement.) Bloom might be contributed by plants in any of these three categories.

VERTICAL ACCENTS typically include shrubs, vines on trellises, and tall, flowering plants (including such bulbs as iris and lilies), as well as dramatic choices like New Zealand flax, small palms, ornamental grasses, and some cacti.

This generously proportioned Asian urn calls for dramatic plantings—sago palms for vertical interest, bright bougainvillea to fill in, and cascading ivy, following the container curves, to soften the arrangement. Design: Jean Manocchio.

FILLERS are low or mounding plants, usually small annuals (such as primroses and dwarf French marigolds) and perennials (including various sages, Mexican daisy, and catmint, to name a few).

CASCADING PLANTS can be found among ivies, vinca, lobelia, spider plant, and numerous others.

MATCHING PLANTS AND POT

Consider the shape of the container, too, to help you decide whether the elements you're considering are compatible. A container with a rounded shape, such as the terra-cotta bowl in the photo at right, would lend itself to a rounded or mounding arrangement of plants, while a long, low trough like the one shown below needs plants of mixed heights so they won't look like a row of soldiers at attention. Square boxes often look best planted with something tall—a small tree, a shrub, or a vine—underplanted with fillers or cascading plants to soften the look. A standard flowerpot, tall or low, is perhaps the most versatile shape of all. It can be planted in a fan shape, with a rounded crown, or even with vertical accents surrounded by low, mounding plants and cascaders.

An unusual container like the giant jar on the facing page calls for creative design solutions. In this arrangement, the fan-shaped palm echoes the rounded shape of the jar; the cascading plants soften and balance the arrangement.

Plants have a style, pots have a style. When you combine them, you want to be sure the two are compatible. A loose, informal mixed "bouquet" of annuals spilling out of a weathered wooden tub looks just right; the same plants would look out of place in a classic Chinese ceramic jar. But a bold, sculptural planting—a palm, perhaps, or a Japanese maple—would suit the Chinese jar perfectly.

Decide whether you want to emphasize the pot, the plant, or both. In general, ornate or particularly distinctive containers should feature simple plantings—broadleafed foliage plants or a shrub—that let the pot be the star. To show off bright, boldleafed plants, choose plainer pots. To make the biggest statement you can, go for the biggest pot you can afford or accommodate gracefully in the space you have.

A rounded nosegay of yellow violas, white marguerites, and purple lobelia provides just the right note of casual charm in this whimsical footed terra-cotta bowl. Design: Jane Hendrix.

A study in form, a rectangular trough is planted with gray-green mounds of licorice plant *(Helichrysum petiolare* 'Variegatum') and lamb's ears *(Stachys byzantina)*. Scarlet and magenta geraniums, kalanchoe, and primula contribute colorful vertical accents. Design: Sydney Baumgartner.

Notations accompanying the plant lists in the following pages let you know how much sunlight and water the arrangement needs for best performance.

"Full sun" means plants grow best with unobstructed sunlight all day long or almost all day. "Part shade" means plants need some shade—half the day or at least 3 hours during the hottest part of the day. "Shade" indicates little or no direct sunlight.

"Regular water" means to water enough that soil doesn't dry out, but not so much that it stays soggy. "Moderate water" indicates less than regular moisture. "Ample water" means plants require constantly moist soil.

USING COLOR

Playing with color is one of the most rewarding aspects of putting together a container planting. The challenge is choosing flower and foliage colors that work together to create visual harmony.

Your palette may be bold or subtle, bright and sunny or cool and restful. "Hot" colors may be found in either flowers or foliage—the intense pink of bougainvillea bracts, the bright yellow and gold of marigolds, the red and pink of coleus. The same is true of "cool" colors, from the blue globe of a hydrangea's blossoms to the quiet gray-green of sage leaves.

Earth tones

Variegation in both flowers and foliage can be used to give container arrangements extra color interest. Many hostas and ivies, for instance, have multicolored leaves; and such flowers as pansies can give you more than a single shot of color.

Don't be afraid to experiment with new color combinations. For starters, you might try one of these four basic approaches:

Mass flowers of one color for simplicity and drama. Use all the same flowers, or different flowers of the same color.

Plant several shades of one color together for subtle plays of dark against light.

Combine cool pastels with lavender and gray-green grasses or other foliage.

Mix hot colors such as bright reds and yellows for "vibrating" color impact.

Keep it simple when you combine colors. Limit the overall scheme to no more than three or four compatible colors. Let foliage plants and airy filler plants in neutral shades help to make a transition between plants with stronger color. Or let the strong-colored foliage of one plant act as a dramatic contrast to the flower color of another.

When you're shopping for plants, do what many plant designers do to try out color combinations: select one plant you love and walk around the nursery with it. Hold it up against various other flowering and foliage plants, and group several plants so you can judge the effect. You may be surprised by the combinations you end up liking—and you'll be better able to visualize how the finished planting will look.

TRICKS WITH WHITE AND GRAY. When it comes to using color, white and gray can be neat "tricks-up-the sleeve" for a savvy gardener.

In flowers or as markings on foliage, white reflects light more than any other color. It's a valuable color enhancer that strengthens the colors of anything planted near it, harmonizes with pastels, and plays up the richness of dark or bright colors. White is also the garden "peacemaker." Flowers that would clash if planted directly next to each other get along beautifully if separated by white. White brightens shady spots and gray days. And when twilight falls, a white container planting fairly glows.

Gray is the real diplomat of the color garden. Found mostly in foliage plants, gray brightens pastels and moderates the heat of bright colors. Like white, gray creates har-

Hot colors

Cool pastels

monious transitions between clashing colors and can tie together potentially disparate elements. Some silvery grays have a luminosity of their own that can light up the garden on dull days and shine in the moonlight.

ADDING TEXTURE

A plant's texture can be every bit as important to a design as its color. Leaves and flower petals may be fine or coarse, their structure dainty or bold, their form strap-shaped or feathery. They may be glossy or matte-surfaced, fuzzy or slick, bumpy or smooth.

Plants with small leaves or leaflets (like English ivy and maidenhair fern) and plants with many tiny flowers (like lobelia and Mexican daisy) are *fine-textured* in appearance. These will be best appreciated in an arrangement that will be viewed close up. For drama, and for containers that will be seen from a distance, choose *coarse-textured* plants—those with large, bold leaves or flowers. The spiky leaves of New Zealand flax, the round pompons of hydrangeas, or the long shapes of angel's trumpet flowers are real attention-getters.

Be aware, too, that matte-finish foliage or flower petals recede a bit visually, while glossy or shiny surfaces reflect light, brightening up a darker arrangement.

You can combine textures for an interesting effect, balancing dainty elements with bold ones, rough textures with smooth ones. Keep texture in mind as you walk around the nursery shopping for plants; try out various combinations together.

DESIGNING A MIXED CONTAINER

You've considered plant choices—size and form, color and texture—and thought about the containers they'll go in. Now it's time to put it all together.

One way to go about creating a container design is to start with a *foundation plant*—a perennial, shrub, or tree—with foliage that will look good all the time and provide a foil for colorful flowers. Citrus, New Zealand flax, or sago palm, for example, could all be used as foundation plants. A foundation plant may also serve as a *vertical accent* in your arrangement.

Next select a couple of flowering plants as *fillers* for the arrangement. These could be annuals or perennials or both, in shades of one color or in contrasting colors. Add one or two *cascading plants*—perhaps a foliage plant like ivy and a flowering plant, in shades and textures compatible with the others you've chosen.

When you plant, first put in the foundation plant (if you're using one) or vertical accents; then fill in with the other plants. As a general rule, taller plants go in the center or at the back of the pot (if it will be viewed only from the front), and middle-height fillers get tucked in around them. Cascaders and low-growing plants go around the outer edges. To try out your arrangement, set plants in place inside the container right in their nursery pots. (If the container is deep, add some soil to bring the plants up to viewing level.) That way you can make design adjustments without having to dig anything up.

For specific instructions on how to plant, see pages 100–101.

Spiky dracaena is foundation plant and vertical accent in this design; white nicotiana and purple heliotrope provide floral filler and color, while trailing ivy geranium cascades down container sides. Design: Ben Hammontree.

HOW LONG WILL IT LAST?

How long can you expect to keep a container arrangement going? The answer depends on your climate and the plants you've chosen. Most planted pots will carry over four seasons only in areas where there is little or no frost. (See pages 106–107 for suggestions for overwintering pots where winter brings some frost.)

A container "stuffed" with plants looks beautifully lush and full. But you can't realistically expect such an arrangement to last for more than a season— plants this closely packed compete for space and nutrients. A pot can also be crowded simply because plants have grown. To keep them going, you can give perennials, shrubs, and trees a "tune-up" as described on pages 110–111. Bulbs can be saved to bloom again, too—see page 109. Some plants, such as ferns, can be repotted as house plants.

SEASON-TO-SEASON POT

The challenge: to create a garden-in-miniature (in one container) that will bloom and look gorgeous all year round. Can it be done? As these pictures demonstrate, the answer is an emphatic "yes"! The secret is simple: you build your design around an arrangement of shrubs and foliage plants, then fill in during the year with annuals and bulbs. Through the seasons, the color palette evolves from a medley of reds, pinks, and golds to a sunny mix of reds and oranges.

In very mild climates, you can keep the foundation plants in this container garden going strong from fall through the following summer. If you live where it gets cold in winter or very hot in summer, follow the same basic plan but combine plants more suitable to your particular climate zone. Opt for dwarf and compact shrubs where possible, so they won't outgrow the space quickly.

You'll need a large container—at least 14 inches deep and 16 inches across—to make your year-round planting successful. The soil volume gives roots of tightly packed plants room to grow and offers more insulation against heat and frost than they'd have in a smaller pot.

PUTTING IT ALL TOGETHER

Start in the fall by planting the shrubs and the New Zealand flax in the center of the pot (or toward the back, if the container will be viewed only from the front). You can set plants close together, since this arrangement is designed to last just a year. Around the outer edges of the pot, plant bulbs and cool-season annuals.

Spring will bring the tulips' fresh touch to the arrangement; when they fade, it will be time to replace cool-season annuals with warm-season choices. (Dig out and discard the tulips; or let the foliage die back, then dig and store as described on page 109.)

The success of this container depends partly on permanent plants staying in scale, so you shouldn't feed them much. At most, mix a little controlled-release fertilizer into the potting mix at planting time. Be vigilant about picking off faded flowers and dead leaves. When you come to the end of the year's cycle, you can set the permanent plants out in your garden and start with all-new plants for the following year. Or, if the plants are healthy and you want to continue using them in the container, prune roots and replant as shown on page 111.

Designs: Kathleen N. Brenzel

SEASON-TO-SEASON DROP-INS

A quick way to add seasonal color to a year-round pot is to use the "drop-in" method. With this technique, you dig a hole in the center of the large pot when you first plant it. The hole should accommodate a nursery pot (4-inch or 1-gallon size, depending on the size of your main container). Drop in a pot of annuals or bulbs (depending on the season), then plant your permanent plants around it.

When the plant in the center fades, you can simply lift it out, in its nursery pot, and replace it with a new plant in the same size pot.

The cycle begins in autumn (RIGHT); permanent plants are set in place, and annuals and bulbs are planted around them. After winter primulas fade, (FAR RIGHT), springtime tulips come on strong. In the summer pot (ABOVE), warm-season annuals bloom in fiery reds and oranges.

WINTER POT

THE PLANTS

☼ ◑ Full sun/part shade in heat
💧 Regular water

PERMANENT PLANTS:

1 AZALEA

2 HEAVENLY BAMBOO
(*Nandina domestica*)

3 LILY-OF-THE-VALLEY SHRUB
(*Pieris japonica*)

4 MEXICAN ORANGE
(*Choisya ternata*)

5 NEW ZEALAND FLAX
(*Phormium tenax*)

6 OREGON GRAPE
(*Mahonia aquifolium*)

BULBS:

7 TULIP

ANNUALS:

8 BLANKET FLOWER
(*Gaillardia*)

9 FRENCH MARIGOLD
(*Tagetes patula*)

10 PRIMROSE
(*Primula obconica*)

11 VIOLA
(*Viola cornuta*)

12 ZINNIA

Autumn pot   Winter pot   Spring pot   Summer pot

PINK LACE

Perfect for dressing up a partially shaded spot, this lovely arrangement combines flowers and attractive foliage in varied shades of pink and green. It's all selected with texture, as well as color, in mind. The dainty foliage of the maidenhair fern picks up the small-scale charm of the lacecap hydrangea florets, while the subtle speckled pink of the polka-dot plant is a perfect foil for the hydrangea's brilliant pink.

Plants are packed into a 13-inch Italian terra-cotta pot, so that the effect is instantly full and lavish. When these plants have filled out to the point of overcrowding, they'll need to be cut back and repotted. You can keep this container arrangement growing over more than one season in a climate that's mild and frost-free year-round. Otherwise, you could treat it as a one-season display and repot the fern, pink polka-dot plant, and snow bush as house plants, as they're often used. The hydrangea could be planted out in the garden or (in subzero regions) overwintered indoors.

Design: Jean Manocchio

THE PLANTS

☼ PART SHADE

◖ REGULAR WATER

1 LACECAP HYDRANGEA
(Hydrangea macrophylla)

2 MAIDENHAIR FERN
(Adiantum)

3 PINK POLKA-DOT PLANT
(Hypoestes phyllostachya)

4 SNOW BUSH
(Breynia disticha)

CONTAINER COMPANIONS

Containers planted with "mixed bouquets" featuring multiple plants certainly can be spectacular. But a container arrangement doesn't have to be complicated to have impact. Often a simple pairing of two plants in a pot has a sum-total effect greater than its parts would have in separate containers.

Variations on this theme are almost endless; let your own sense of color and form be your guide. Try some unexpected combinations—but do be sure to choose two plants with the same light, water, and soil requirements. Here are a few ideas to get you started:

COMBINE FLOWERING PLANTS of equal importance, such as white cyclamen and pink primroses, chosen for their complementary colors and/or textures.

PAIR A BRIGHT FLOWERING PLANT such as a tuberous begonia with a fern or other lush green foliage plant to set off the blossom color.

OVERPLANT BULBS with flowering annuals or perennials; these will provide ongoing color and foliage interest before and after the bulbs bloom in their midst.

UNDERPLANT a shrub, small tree, or other tall plant with a low-growing or trailing one, to balance the shape and soften the edges of the pot.

TOP: Tree-trained bougainvillea is underplanted with a frilly petticoat of alyssum. Design: Stephen Adams.

RIGHT: Spiky New Zealand flax makes a surprising partner for kalanchoe. Design: Jean Manocchio.

LEFT: Exotic dwarf 'Heartbeat' Oriental lilies are paired with creeping phlox.

THE PLANTS

☼ Full sun

◑◑ Moderate to
regular water

1 COREOPSIS

2 GERANIUM
(*Pelargonium*)

3 GROUND IVY
(*Glechoma hederacea*)

4 SWAN RIVER DAISY
(*Brachycome*)

5 VERBENA
(*Verbena hybrida*)

CLASSIC BOUQUET

Spilling over with bloom, this bouquet-in-a-pot is a charming mosaic of small-scale flowers in rainbow hues; the myriad points of color seem to sparkle in the sun. The texture of the plantings is light, airy, and delicate. Clouds of flowers float above and outside the boundaries of the simple terra-cotta pot, while small-leafed ground ivy trails over the pot's edge, carrying out the scale and mood.

This one-season arrangement will grow lush and full in the bright summer sun. The key to keeping it looking its best is regular deadheading and shaping throughout the growing season, so that the blooms are abundant and dense, and the plant shapes stay full yet controlled.

Design: Sue Rohwer

VAN GOGH REVISITED

An old-fashioned summer favorite—the sunflower—gets star billing in this sunny composition of flowers that looks as if it could have come off a Van Gogh canvas. Look for shorter-growing varieties of sunflowers, so they'll stay in scale with the other plants in the container and won't outgrow their space.

The color theme of the whole arrangement evokes images of long, golden afternoons. It's carried out with French marigolds and creeping zinnias as well as the sunflower; white sweet alyssum adds a light, frothy touch. A simple terra-cotta pot is just right for this casual, playful combination of summer plants.

Design: Peggy Henry

THE PLANTS

☼ FULL SUN
🌢 REGULAR WATER

1 CREEPING ZINNIA
(Sanvitalia procumbens)

2 FRENCH MARIGOLD
(Tagetes patula)

3 SUNFLOWER
(Helianthus)

4 SWEET ALYSSUM
(Lobularia maritima)

RISING ABOVE THE ORDINARY

Florists know all the tricks of flower arranging—a tall blossom here, a shorter bloom there. These contrasting heights help attract and delight the eye.

The same principle applies to groupings of plants in containers. A cluster of pots at ankle level is not nearly so interesting as a collection with varied heights. Just as you try to vary height when you position plants within a single container, you can create greater impact by giving the same sort of structural design to your groupings of pots.

Varying your container sizes is one way to vary the heights of your plants somewhat. And you can also use all sorts of props that you may already have on hand. Set a container of plants atop an upturned empty pot, or stack bricks or tiles to raise a container. Display a container on a low garden table or an old chair, with other pots grouped nearby on the ground.

Consider the possibilities offered by stairsteps, the edges of raised decks, even the crooks of trees. A ladder can make a great multilevel plant stand. So can a tree stump, a bench, blocks of wood, an upturned bucket, a child's wagon. Just be sure to protect surfaces from moisture if they need it, and be sure raised containers are securely positioned.

TOP: Raised to different levels, pots of hydrangeas, ageratum, streptocarpus, ferns, and Persian violet create a mounded garden on a shady patio.

RIGHT: Grouping pots of all sizes instantly creates eye-catching height variation.

ABOVE: A centerpiece tree gives vertical interest to pot grouping; some plants are lifted on stacked tiles.

LEFT: Hidden inside pipes sold for lining chimneys, stacked wood pieces or upended empty pots raise plants in pots. Design: Richard William Wogisch.

BELOW LEFT: Wooden posts of different heights bring pots into close viewing range.

BELOW RIGHT: Containers get a boost from stairsteps and newel post.

FOUNTAIN OF GRASSES

Strawberry pots look lovely when planted with cascades of foliage and berries. Plant them with unexpected choices like the soft, billowy grasses shown here, and their impact can be dramatic indeed.

Shape and texture are the hallmarks of this unique arrangement. Planted in the top of the pot are arching sprays of purple fountain grass, soft spikes of golden needle grass, and mounding, round-leafed licorice plant. The pockets are overflowing with blue fescue, blue-violet dwarf cup flower, snow-in-summer, and white sweet alyssum. With sunlight playing over the soft and graceful forms, the effect is that of a fountain of subtle color and texture.

This arrangement started with 1-gallon containers of purple fountain grass, Mexican feather grass, and licorice plant and a cell-pack of each of the other plants. For other suggested grasses that make good container plants, and for basic care instructions for grasses, see page 41.

This is a spring-to-fall pot—the fountain and feather grasses will die back in winter, even in mild climates, and will need to be sheared back in spring before new growth starts. Shear back the dwarf cup flower in spring, too. Replace the annuals—the snow-in-summer and sweet alyssum; the licorice plant is a tender perennial that can be treated as an annual. Tuck the pot out of sight for the winter if you want to keep it going, or replace all the plants for a new look.

Design: Bud Stuckey

THE PLANTS
☼ FULL SUN
💧 REGULAR WATER

1 BLUE FESCUE
(*Festuca ovina* 'Glauca')

2 DWARF CUP FLOWER
(*Nierembergia hippomanica violacea* 'Purple Robe')

3 LICORICE PLANT
(*Helichrysum petiolare*)

4 MEXICAN FEATHER GRASS/
TEXAS NEEDLE GRASS
(*Stipa tenuissima*)

5 PURPLE FOUNTAIN GRASS
(*Pennisetum setaceum* 'Rubrum')

6 SNOW-IN-SUMMER
(*Cerastium tomentosum*)

7 SWEET ALYSSUM
(*Lobularia maritima*)

PLANTING A POCKET POT

No matter what you're planting in a pocket planter, choose a pot with generously flared, cup-shaped pockets; they'll hold moisture better than very narrow, slit-like pockets.

Plant the pot tier by tier. Fill the bottom with planting mix up to the first tier of planting holes; then add your plants, spreading the roots out on the soil and threading the plants gently through the pockets from inside the pot. Fill in with soil. Continue planting the pockets, moving up toward the top. Finally, put in the top plants.

FOR EFFICIENT WATERING...

One way to assure even watering throughout a strawberry pot (or other very deep container) is to make a "watering pipe" from a length of ¾-inch PVC pipe about 4 inches longer than the height of the pot. Drill ¼-inch holes through the pipe about every 2 inches and cap the bottom end. Stand the pipe in the center of the pot (leave the drainage hole free) and plant the pot. To water after planting, water the soil on top and in each planting pocket; then add water through the pipe opening.

CONTEMPORARY CLASSIC

A bold asymmetrical shape makes this container arrangement a standout. Careful plant selection and placement create the dramatic look. The colors here are subtle; it's the overall form and combination of textures that are the focus for this design.

Shrubby Mexican sage, mounding fountain grass, and frilly-leaved plume poppy anchor the design with their rounded shapes, while the airy flower stalks of verbena give it height and lightness. The red-flowered sedum adds balance to both the color and shape of the arrangement.

Since plants are closely packed, this arrangement of perennials and shrubs is intended to last just for a single spring-to-fall growing season. Then individual plants can be moved into their own containers or planted in the ground.

Design: Jan Cole,
Orchard Nursery and Florist

THE PLANTS

☼ FULL SUN

💧 MODERATE WATER

1 DWARF FOUNTAIN GRASS
   (Pennisetum orientale)

2 MEXICAN BUSH SAGE
   (Salvia leucantha)

3 PLUME POPPY
   (Macleaya cordata)

4 SEDUM
   (Sedum sieboldii 'Ruby Glow'*)*

5 ST. CATHERINE'S LACE
   (Eriogonum giganteum) *

6 VERBENA
   (Verbena bonariensis)

*This plant is a West Coast native; related wild buckwheat species, with yellow flowers, grow in Virginia and the Rocky Mountains.

SCULPTURE IN A DISH

You don't have to plant on a large scale to enjoy a cactus and succulent garden. This tabletop dish garden shows off a delightful small collection that is a study in shape and form. The plump, globe-shaped cactus is the centerpiece; it will eventually carry a bright flower at the top. Various succulents (a *Sedum* and two *Sempervivum* species) are the frame—some sporting bright flowers, each with an interesting shape and pattern of leaf arrangement.

The container is wide and quite shallow—most cacti and succulents are shallow-rooted, making them ideal for dish gardens. Small smooth stones are tucked among the plants to give the composition a found-in-nature look.

Grow this arrangement in the sun during warm weather, sheltering it from any heavy rains; in freezing weather, bring it indoors to a well-lighted window to enjoy all winter. For tips on planting and care of cacti and succulents, see page 47.

THE PLANTS

☼ FULL SUN

◗◗● MODERATE TO REGULAR WATER

1 HOUSELEEKS
  (*Sempervivum* species)

2 MAMMILLARIA CACTUS

3 PORK AND BEANS
  (*Sedum rubrotinctum*)

SUNSHINE IN SHADE

● ◐ SHADE/PART SHADE
● REGULAR WATER

THE PLANTS

1 BOSTON FERN
 (*Nephrolepis exaltata* 'Bostoniensis')

2 FLOWERING MAPLE
 (*Abutilon hybridum*)

3 IMPATIENS
 (*Impatiens wallerana*)

4 LILY TURF
 (*Liriope muscari*)

5 TUBEROUS BEGONIA

MADE FOR SHADE

Not every container garden has to bask in brilliant sunlight in order to shine. If your deck, porch, or patio is shaded, you can create container combinations every bit as colorful as their sun-drenched counterparts—as evidenced by the three arrangements shown here.

When you shop for shade plants at the nursery, head first for the lath house—that's where shade-loving plants will be on display. Then take a look at the house plant section. The plants shown on these two pages can help you get started.

Plants in full or partial shade don't need watering as often as pots in full sun. Depending on the pot's porosity and on temperature and wind factors, you can probably get away with watering only every 2 or 3 days, instead of daily. If you add polymers to the soil at planting time (see page 99), you can reduce the need for water even more.

One thing to be especially watchful for in shaded containers is the presence of slugs and snails—they thrive in moist, cool conditions.

SUNSHINE IN SHADE

Proving that even shade-loving plants can add warm and sunny color to the garden or patio, big blooms of yellow and red tuberous begonias glow amid lush green foliage plants. Red flowering maple and impatiens blossoms add more spots of color. The interplay of leaf textures adds an extra dimension of interest to this well-designed pot. In cold-winter areas, overwinter the pot indoors, or treat it as you would an annuals pot and start again in the spring with new plants.

LEAFY SYMPHONY

Foliage alone provides all the color and form necessary for this knockout composition of color and pattern. The bold green leaves of hosta make a dramatic statement; the variegated foliage of houttuynia and ivy, in colors both brilliant and subtle, enliven the composition, while the coleus chimes in with its own deep red notes.

Pinch and trim the coleus, ivy, and houttuynia as needed to keep the composition balanced. Although all these plants are technically perennials, the coleus is generally treated as an annual; replace it with a new plant when it fades.

Design: Peggy Henry

WOODLAND CHARMER

● ☼ SHADE/PART SHADE
● REGULAR WATER

THE PLANTS

1 AMETHYST FLOWER
   (*Browallia*)

2 DUMB CANE
   (*Dieffenbachia maculata*
   'Rudolph Roehrs')

3 ENGLISH IVY
   (*Hedera helix*)

4 FUCHSIA
   (*Fuchsia hybrida*
   'Gartenmeister Bonstedt')

5 IMPATIENS
   (*Impatiens wallerana*)

6 SWEET WOODRUFF
   (*Galium odoratum*)

WOODLAND CHARMER

Dainty textures and subtle colors give this planting a woodland air. The green foliage and starlike leaf shapes of ivy and fragrant sweet woodruff lend a suggestion of the forest floor; they soften the pot's edge with their cascading growth. Fuchsia adds a vertical accent as well as contributing blossoms, which blend nicely with the pinks and intense blues of the other flowering plants. The dieffenbachia's foliage in pale and dark shades of green is an effective accent.

LEAFY SYMPHONY

● ☼ SHADE/PART SHADE
● ●● REGULAR TO AMPLE
   WATER

THE PLANTS

1 COLEUS

2 ENGLISH IVY
   (*Hedera helix*)

3 HOUTTUYNIA
   (*H. cordata* 'Variegata')

4 PLANTAIN LILY
   (*Hosta*)

THE PLANTS

☼ PART SHADE
💧 AMPLE WATER

1 BLUE STAR CREEPER
   (*Laurentia fluviatilis*)

2 COLEUS

3 HELIOTROPE
   (*Heliotropium arborescens*)

4 IMPATIENS
   (*Impatiens wallerana*)

5 NEEDLEPOINT IVY
   (*Hedera helix* 'Needlepoint')

6 PINK POLKA-DOT PLANT
   (*Hypoestes phyllostachya*)

AERIAL GARDEN

A cool, airy look makes this hanging basket a perfect summer "ornament" for a shady balcony or porch. Its pretty pastel colors and dainty textures bring to mind a setting replete with wicker chairs, lemonade, and light summer breezes.

The mix of delicate blue star creeper, miniature ivy, impatiens in three soft shades, heliotrope, and other plants is carefully planned for harmony and balance of color, shape, and texture. All the plants are small-leafed, with dainty flowers, to create a light, lacy look. They're kept pinched back as needed to form a round, full ball shape; the ivy provides a graceful cascading touch. The cool greens (including lime green coleus), whites (heliotrope), and quiet shades of pink blend subtly with one another.

It's all planted in an 18-inch-wide wire basket, lined with sphagnum moss, then planted through the sides and across the top in extra-lightweight soil (see instructions on facing page). Plants are set quite close so they'll fill in well. Because the container's open all around, it will need to be watered frequently.

The heliotrope for this arrangement was propagated from stem cuttings, since it's not typically sold small enough to insert into a hanging basket.

Design: Kerry Zerr

PLANTING A WIRE BASKET

Want to look eye-to-eye with some black-eyed Susan vines or fairy primroses—or even leaf lettuce or green beans? A hanging wire mesh basket lets you do just that. Planted on all sides, this kind of container can create a lush ball of flowers or foliage, or keep vegetables above the reach of many garden pests.

Traditionally, wire mesh baskets are lined with sphagnum moss and filled with potting soil. Today you also have the option of simplifying the process by using drop-in liners available from nurseries, garden centers, and mail-order garden businesses. You'll find them in both plastic-lined polyester (which cuts down on moisture loss) and such natural materials as cocoa fiber. Or you can make a liner yourself from burlap (to hold the soil in place) or other materials. Just cut slits to accommodate plants, then follow the same steps you'd use to plant a basket lined with moss.

Select a wire basket 12 inches or more in diameter, use lightweight potting mix (see pages 98–99), and plant cell-pack–size seedlings. Here's how to proceed.

1 Push soaking-wet green sphagnum moss through the basket mesh from the inside to make a lining that's 1 inch thick, extending 1 inch above the basket rim.

2 Starting from the bottom, poke planting holes 2 to 6 inches apart in the moss. Then insert cell-pack–size plants in the basket's bottom tier, pushing roots through from outside while gently pulling from inside. Add enough soil to cover the plant roots and gently tamp it down. (If you wish, you can add a teaspoon of soil polymer at the bottom of the basket to help retain moisture near roots.)

3 Continue planting and adding soil in tiers, filling in the top of the basket with soil last and adding 1 or more plants on top, depending on the size of the basket. Water gently.

CARE AND FEEDING

A moss-lined basket will dry out quickly, so continue watering it daily as needed—or even more often if the weather's very hot or the basket is exposed to drying winds. (But be careful not to overwater newly planted seedlings; soggy soil can hamper root growth.) Two weeks after planting, apply liquid fertilizer at one-half the recommended monthly amount; continue feeding at half strength every other week. Alternatively, you can add timed-release fertilizer to the soil mix before planting, according to package directions.

FIREBURST

For a different approach to the red/pink color family, try this sun-loving arrangement. Plants of dramatic form and color burst exuberantly from a 20-inch Italian terra-cotta urn. They include the bold, swordlike leaves of variegated New Zealand flax, along with dancing branches of the tropical-looking bougainvillea vine in an intense shade of cherry red. Both spring from a dense bed of purple heliotrope. The whole effect is one of lively motion and sun-baked color. All plants will live from year to year but are frost-tender, so this container would require winter protection in all but the mildest areas.

The bougainvillea shown here can be a vigorous grower. If you want a shrubby type that will stay confined longer, try 'Crimson Jewel,' 'Hawaii,' 'La Jolla,' 'Rosenka,' or 'Temple Fire.' No matter which you plant, you may have to keep it in check with assertive pruning!

Design: Jean Manocchio

THE PLANTS
☼ FULL SUN
💧 MODERATE WATER

1 BOUGAINVILLEA 'BARBARA KARST'

2 HELIOTROPE (*Heliotropium arborescens*)

3 NEW ZEALAND FLAX (*Phormium tenax* 'Maori Maiden')

THE PLANTS

☼ FULL SUN
💧 REGULAR WATER

1 'BUSH GREEN' BASIL

2 CHIVES

3 ITALIAN PARSLEY

4 'LEMON' BASIL

5 'LETTUCE LEAF' BASIL

6 'PURPLE RUFFLES' BASIL

7 'THAI' BASIL

8 VARIEGATED LEMON THYME

DOUBLE-DECKER HERB POT

Herbs are a cook's best friends and a gardener's delight. You'll get double-duty from a potful of herbs with texture and color to please the eye as well as scents and flavors to pique the palate.

This two-tier planting, overflowing with a variety of herbs, was created by stacking one bowl-shaped terra-cotta container atop another. The pots used here are 16 and 24 inches across; whatever sizes you use, just be sure the bottom pot is enough bigger to allow plenty of planting room. Plant taller herbs in the top pot, cascading ones and low, bushy plants in the bottom tier. Fill in with short plants such as chives.

This arrangement concentrates on basils, one of the easiest herbs to grow. Basil thrives in warm and hot weather, producing an abundance of attractive foliage over a long season. Special Italian varieties, dwarf basil from Greece, and basils with lemon, licorice, or clove scents are some intriguing ones to try.

For a fast start, buy herbs in 2- or 4-inch pots. Many kinds, including basil, can also be grown from seed. Pinch back the growing tips of basil plants for bushiness, fertilize regularly, and pinch off flowers.

Design: Lauren Bonar Swezey

WINDOW BOX GARDENS

For an up-close garden view, there's nothing like a window box. Window plantings decorate the inside and outside of a home at the same time. And window boxes are not just for those lacking any other outside access to soil; even gardeners with acres at their command appreciate the intimacy of window boxes.

Garden and home supply stores stock ready-made window boxes in a variety of shapes, sizes, and materials. If you choose wood (or build your own window box), decay-resistant redwood or cedar is especially long-lasting. Painting, staining, or sealing wood will make it last longer (see page 23), or you can waterproof it on the inside with asphalt roofing emulsion or a plastic or metal liner, if you wish. Be sure the window box (and liner, if you use one) has drain holes: a ½- to ¾-inch hole per foot of box length.

INSTALLING A WINDOW BOX

Remember that a window box will be heavy when planted: a cubic foot of potting soil can weigh 90 pounds after watering. Be sure the window box is adequately supported from the bottom; decorative wooden braces, large angle irons screwed into the wall, and custom-made steel or iron brackets all work well.

Anchor the box to the wall so that it won't topple off its supports. You can do this by bolting a pressure-treated 2-by-2 or 2-by-4, slightly shorter than the box length, to the wall, then screwing the back of the box to this horizontal runner. This allows plenty of clearance for drainage and air circulation between box and wall. (You may need a second 2-by-2 or 2-by-4 as a spacer at the bottom of the box.) Don't attach the box directly to a wooden wall or you'll encourage the siding to rot.

To minimize the potential for dry rot, most building codes require that there be at least a 2-inch air

TOP: Brimming with petunias, a simple window box provides country charm. BELOW: rustic box is chock-full of tall viscaria *(Lychinis),* schizanthus, petunias, lobelia, white alyssum, and jasmine. Design: Peggy Quaid.

space between a window box and an outside house wall. If the space is less than 6 inches, galvanized sheet-metal flashing may be required between the wall and the box. Check to see what your local requirements are.

Since window boxes need regular tending, they shouldn't be placed where they're difficult to reach. And if a window swings outward to open, plants directly in front of it might be a problem.

Water must drain away from house walls and foundations, so drainage holes shouldn't be too close to the back of the box. Use a piece of plastic mesh or a layer of gravel in the bottom of the box to keep soil from washing out drain holes.

NEXT, THE PLANTS

After installing your window box comes the fun part—choosing the plants. Just about anything goes—a kitchen garden of culinary herbs, a cottage garden–style mixture of colors and shapes, a monochromatic arrangement (orange nasturtiums, marigolds, and California poppies, for example), or a combination of upright and trailing plants.

Typically, window-box plantings consist of three parts: tall background plants (such as geraniums), low-growing foreground plants (like dwarf marigolds), and trailers to spill out of the box (verbena and ivy, for instance). Almost any plant of fairly modest size is a window box candidate. Just make sure it's suited to your climate and exposure. Begonias, fuchsias, geraniums, impatiens, lobelia, marigolds, petunias, and dusty miller are among the classic summer plants for window boxes.

If you live in a mild climate, you may want to change your window-box plantings three times a year: you could plant annuals for summer; cyclamen, pansies, and ornamental cabbages for winter; and primroses or bulbs for spring. Or combine your blooming seasonal plants with all-year foliage plants such as English ivy.

Plants in a window box need a loose, lightweight potting soil. Most commercial mixes work well. Work a controlled-release fertilizer into the soil mix at planting time, or plan to apply a complete liquid fertilizer every 2 to 4 weeks.

Then comes frequent and thorough watering—perhaps daily or more often in summer, since window boxes tend to be exposed to full sun, drying winds, and the reflected heat of the house. Installing a drip irrigation system will simplify this chore.

Pinch off faded blooms to keep the flowers coming.

Long skeins of ground ivy (Glechoma hederacea) cascade like a waterfall of greenery from window box, setting off bold flower colors of geraniums, marigolds, and trailing lobelia.

Foliage, orange impatiens combine in an understated display.

A MOVEABLE FLORAL FEAST

To create a plantscape that can change with the seasons or on a whim, forego planting directly into the window box. Instead, fill the box with coarse vermiculite, then sink 6-inch (or bigger) containers into that medium. A bonus: the vermiculite helps keep plants from drying out.

THE PLANTS

☀ FULL SUN
💧 REGULAR WATER

1 DWARF GLORIOSA DAISY
   (*Rudbeckia hirta* 'Becky Mix')

2 'NAGAMI' KUMQUAT

3 SCAEVOLA AEMULA
   'BLUE WONDER'

FRUIT AND FLOWERS

A small tree can be the centerpiece of a dramatic large-scale container design. This one features a handsome 'Nagami' kumquat—known in China as a good-luck plant. The kumquat is an excellent, versatile container specimen. It bears loads of sweet, showy fruit; and in spring, it's covered with richly perfumed white blossoms. The dense foliage is attractive, too; here the shrubby plant has been pruned and trained to display a rounded shape atop a single trunk.

The centerpiece tree is underplanted with blooming plants that spill over the container's edges, adding splashes of bold color and giving balance to the design so that it doesn't appear top-heavy.

A planter for a small tree should be at least 18 inches across; this square concrete container is a generous 22 inches.

Because the kumquat is fairly tender (to about 18°F/−8°C), be prepared to move the entire container indoors if you live in a colder-winter area. (In fact, this is one kind of citrus you *can* grow indoors year-round, given bright light and sufficiently moist air.) If your climate allows you to keep this arrangement outdoors all year, the flowering plants can be left in the container. But they are short-lived perennials, often treated as annuals, and will need replacing after a couple of seasons.

Design: Jean Manocchio

SPIRIT OF SUMMER

As bright and exuberant as summer itself, this wooden half-barrel of mixed annual flowers is put together in the spirit of casual fun. Yet careful color choice and arrangement of plants is behind its apparent casualness.

Sunny golden marigolds in two sizes echo one another's shapes and colors—the smaller varieties sparkle along the pot's rim, while the larger pompon shapes dance above. Soft lavender-pink floss flower and hot pink and red petunias fill in the middle tier—they're colorful standouts among the yellow marigolds. A fern asparagus is beginning to make its way over the barrel's edge; as it fills out it will provide soft green texture. And above it all, black-eyed Susans—those quintessential summer flowers—rise tall on slender stems to give the whole picture a loosely triangular shape reminiscent of a casually picked bouquet.

This is an arrangement for a sunny spot—one that's meant to dress up the patio or garden for just one season.

THE PLANTS

☼ FULL SUN

⬤ REGULAR WATER

1 BLACK-EYED SUSAN
(*Rudbeckia hirta*)

2 FERN ASPARAGUS
(*Asparagus setaceus*)

3 FLOSS FLOWER
(*Ageratum houstonianum*)

4 MARIGOLD
(*Tagetes*)

5 PETUNIA

ENSEMBLE PIECE

Flowers and foliage perform in close harmony in this spirited composition. The pale pot color sets off the dramatic patterns of the boldly-veined caladium, sansevieria, and tropical African mask plant as well as vivid flower colors—the trio of scarlet-colored New Guinea impatiens, orange tuberous begonias, and hot pink fuchsias. Flashy, unexpected foliage choices are paired with more familiar container plants for a unique and eye-catching effect.

This mix of annuals and perennials is definitely a mild-weather pot. If you want to save some of the plants when autumn arrives, dig up the begonias and caladium and store the tubers as described for Group 2 bulbs on page 43. The sansevieria and African mask can move indoors as house plants, or they can stay outdoors in no-frost zones—as can the fuchsia.

Design: Tom Peace

THE PLANTS

☼ ◐ FULL SUN/PART SHADE
💧 AMPLE WATER

1 AFRICAN MASK
   (Alocasia amazonica)

2 CALADIUM

3 COLEUS

4 ENGLISH IVY
   (Hedera helix)

5 FUCHSIA
   (Fuchsia hybrida)

6 IMPATIENS
   (New Guinea hybrid)

7 LOBELIA
   (Lobelia erinus)

8 SANSEVIERIA

9 TUBEROUS BEGONIA

THE PLANTS
:☼: PART SHADE
💧 REGULAR WATER

1 LEATHERLEAF FERN
   (Rumohra adiantiformis)

2 LILY-OF-THE-VALLEY
   (Convallaria majalis)

3 VARIEGATED IVY
   (Hedera helix 'Glacier'*)*

SPRINGTIME SIMPLICITY

Simple plant combinations, like this charming springtime arrangement, can be every bit as striking as those with many elements. Here there are just three plants, in simple green and white—yet the combination gives a strong impression of cool woodland serenity.

The wide bowl shape of the terra-cotta pot is perfect for a miniature glade of nodding, sweetly-scented lilies-of-the-valley. Fern and ivy spill over the sides, softening and balancing the composition and adding a wash of fresh green and white.

When the blossoms have faded, the foliage continues to look lush and green, though eventually the lily-of-the-valley leaves will die back. If you want the pot to continue blooming, add a shade-tolerant annual when the lily-of-the-valley blossoms fade.

This container can look attractive for up to two years if you wish to keep it going. Let the lily-of-the-valley leaves dry up in the pot to "refuel" the plant for the next bloom season. They can stay in the pot along with the ivy through the winter if temperatures don't drop below 0°F/−18°C, though you'll need to dig up the fern and bring it indoors in cold areas—or substitute a cold-hardy one.

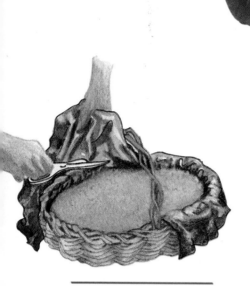

PREPARING A BASKET

Choose a sturdy basket that can support the weight of wet potting mix, and line it with a piece of 3-mil plastic cut from a heavy-duty trash bag; let the plastic drape over the edges. Punch drainage holes in the plastic, using a nail or scissors.

Fill the lined basket with moistened potting mix. Then trim the plastic to just below the basket rim.

GARDEN GIFTS

A big basket or a wooden crate filled with herbs, salad greens, or blooming plants makes a wonderful gift—or a handsome living centerpiece for your own table. Add some dyed eggs to a nest of greens and you have an Easter basket. Or choose blooming plants in colors to complement a particular season.

SPRING SALAD BASKET

The essential ingredient for this basket is a mix of salad greens, known as *mesclun*. You can buy a premixed blend of seeds or mix your own. Many greens will germinate within days of planting, and you can start harvesting in 2 to 4 weeks.

For piquant flavors, try arugula, chicory, mizuna, red mustard, and curly cress. To mellow the mix, add loose-leaf and romaine lettuces. You can also add herbs and edible flowers (such as nasturtiums) from cell-packs or 2-inch pots.

1 In a lined basket filled with potting mix, plant any herb or flower seedlings that you are using, positioning trailing plants close to edge.

2 If you are blending your own mesclun, mix seeds together before planting. Scatter seeds thinly over the soil surface, then cover with a ¼-inch layer of potting mix.

3 Water to keep soil moist until seeds sprout. (To encourage quick germination in a seeds-only basket, cover with plastic until seeds start to sprout.) Then place basket in a sunny spot.

MIXED HERB BASKET

For even quicker results, plant an herb basket using purchased herbs from 2- and 4-inch pots. Select herbs for their textural interest as well as their fragrance and flavor. The basket shown at right combines nasturtiums, two kinds of parsley, chives, oregano, thyme, and rosemary. Other possibilities include basil, chervil, cilantro, and sweet marjoram.

Position low-growing and trailing herbs close to the sides of the prepared basket (see far left). Use tall, upward growers such as Italian parsley and sweet basil in the center.

HERB GARDEN IN A CRATE

A wooden crate such as those sold for storing audio tapes or CDs makes a good-looking container for a small herb garden. Since the crate is lined only with sphagnum moss, it will drain freely. Place it where water staining won't be a problem.

The crate shown here is planted with three herbs from 2-inch pots. Deeper crates can hold slightly larger plants. Choose small-scale herbs such as chives, cilantro, parsley, sage, or tarragon. Here's how to proceed:

1 Line the sides and bottom of the crate with moist sphagnum moss, pressing it in firmly.

2 Add a layer of potting mix.

3 Knock the herbs out of their nursery containers and space them evenly in the crate.

4 Fill in around the plants with more potting mix, and press a thin layer of sphagnum moss over the soil to help hold in moisture. Water and place the crate in a sunny spot.

ONGOING CARE

For best success, a basket or crate of herbs or greens should be placed outdoors where it gets at least 4 hours of sun every day. Position flower baskets according to their particular exposure needs.

Water daily (or as needed), letting the water run through freely. To counteract the leaching effect of frequent watering, feed every 2 weeks with a complete liquid fertilizer at half strength.

Harvest herbs and greens liberally to keep plants compact and bushy, and trim away yellowed leaves and leaves that shade other plants. When wide-spreading plants get too big, cut them back.

If you live in a mild-winter region, you can keep a basket going all year. Replace summer herbs with others that like cool weather. In the fall, pull out annual herbs such as basil and replace with cilantro, Italian parsley, or leaf lettuce.

GLOWING COLOR

The rich colors of this plant combination positively glow in the golden light of an early autumn afternoon. Fluffy-textured Myers asparagus—the centerpiece of the composition—is an intense lime green; surrounding it are orange snapdragons, purple alyssum, and the deep blue-violet of trailing lobelia. The composition boasts interesting shapes as well as colors; the spikes of the Myers asparagus and snapdragons contrast with the round forms of the alyssum and lobelia.

This is an example of a highly flexible composition that lends itself to experimentation. The ornamental asparagus is the permanent resident of this 22-inch terra-cotta pot; its companions can be replaced in another season with different annuals and trailing plants. A favorite fixture in the Sunset gardens, this arrangement was originally planted with a Myers asparagus, some ivy, and some sweet alyssum. Over a five-year period other plants were added and annuals came and went, but the ornamental asparagus remained at center stage.

The arrangement will thrive outdoors year-round in a mild climate. In cold-winter areas, the Myers asparagus can be brought indoors as a house plant.

Design: Kim Haworth

THE PLANTS

☼ ◑ FULL SUN/PART SHADE
💧 REGULAR WATER

1 MYERS ASPARAGUS
(Asparagus densiflorus 'Myers'*)*

2 SNAPDRAGON
(Antirrhinum majus)

3 SWEET ALYSSUM
(Lobularia maritima)

4 TRAILING LOBELIA
(Lobelia erinus)

A LIVING HOLIDAY TREE

If a Christmas tree is part of your household's traditions, you may want to consider making it a living one. An evergreen in a container can come indoors for a week or so every December, then return outdoors for the rest of the year.

Firs, spruces, and pines of many kinds are available as living Christmas trees. Popular types vary in their growth rates, shape, height, and width—ask at the nursery about the sizes and characteristics of different trees, and find out which type grows best in your climate.

If you're buying a tree just before the holidays, try to find one that has lived in its nursery container for a year or more. A tree only recently dug from a field has probably left some of its roots behind and will not be as able to stand the shock of its indoor stay.

INDOORS/OUTDOORS

Acclimate your tree gradually, especially where outdoor temperatures dip below 20°F/−7°C at night. Leave it in an interim spot—a windowed garage, porch, or basement—for several days. The day before bringing the tree inside, soak it thoroughly.

In the house, place the tree well away from heat sources. Use a drip saucer beneath the tree. For slow and safe watering, set ice cubes on the soil every few days.

Plan to return the tree to the outdoors after an indoor stay of a week to 10 days. If you live in a cold climate, move your tree first to a transitional location, the same as when you brought it indoors.

If the tree has spent more than a year in its pot, it can safely stay outside in just about any location, in full sun or partial shade. However, a fairly recent transplant should be protected from hot afternoon sun and drying winds.

Water regularly, and apply a fertilizer once in spring and again in summer. If the tree is still in a small or medium-size container, repot it into a slightly larger container when its roots get crowded. Do this in spring or summer, scoring the outside of the rootball with a knife if roots are matted. If a tree in a big pot is rootbound, remove it from the container and shave off several inches of roots and soil from the sides and bottom of the rootball, then return the tree to its pot with new soil.

This tree is for the birds! When your tree's back outdoors, why not decorate it with treats for feathered friends? This one offers dried fruit, corn, cranberries, and pine cones covered with peanut butter and seeds. Design: Bud Stuckey.

CONDENSED VERSION

You can buy miniature living Christmas trees in gallon cans and even *really* tiny ones in 2- to 6-inch-wide containers. Bunched together, several can suggest a little forest.

To remain healthy, a mini needs bright indirect light indoors. Don't let pots sit in water, and don't let the soil dry out. Acclimate plants to the outdoors after the holidays by placing them on the patio or in another protected area for a few weeks. Transplant into larger pots as needed.

HOLIDAY BOUQUETS

When the winter holidays approach, many of us get the urge to "deck the halls," indoors and out, with special displays of winter greenery and lights. If you live in a mild-winter climate, your outdoor containers can get into the act. With a little creativity you can make them showcases for bright and cheerful holiday arrangements.

Living bouquets can be put together from pots of nursery plants for an almost instant effect. Add cut evergreen boughs for an extra seasonal touch. You can also create the same sort of arrangement as a holiday gift basket—see page 90 for instructions for assembling one.

For dramatic impact by your front door or on your deck or patio, choose a pot that's generously-sized—at least 12 to 14 inches across. If you plan to set pots on your steps, be sure the the pot base is no wider than the step.

PICKING A PALETTE AND PLANTS

You can mix different colors for a festive look or limit your palette to shades of one color for a more sophisticated approach. If you're after traditional Christmas colors, use flowers and foliage in tones of gold, green, red, silver gray, and white. Red-and-white color schemes are naturals, especially with greenery to set them off. An all-white scheme accented with green looks dramatic.

You want instant good looks, so buy well-established nursery plants in 4-inch, 6-inch, and 1-gallon sizes. Choose foliage plants, like shrubs and ferns, with attractive shapes, textures,

BELOW: Pine cones, cut greens, and red ribbon add holiday cheer to this planting of heath, English primrose, *Primula obconica,* and red kalanchoe.

BELOW RIGHT: This arrangement will look appealing long past the season's end. The combination of spiky *Iris foetidissima* and lacy ornamental asparagus *(Asparagus retrofractus)* creates textural interest. Variegated ivy trails over the edge, and cyclamen adds that all-important splash of color.

All-white plantings offer a bright welcome for the holidays. These terra-cotta pots hold violas, primroses, camellias, and paperwhite narcissus.

A SELECTION OF HOLIDAY PLANTS

FOR FLOWERS

Azalea (rose or white)
Camellia (red or white)
Cyclamen (red, pink, or white)
Heath (rosy red *Erica canaliculata* 'Rosea')

Kalanchoe (red or gold)
Poinsettia (red, pink, or off-white)
Primrose (red or white)
Viola (white)

FOR FOLIAGE

Aucuba japonica
English ivy (*Hedera helix*)
Holly fern (*Cyrtomium falcatum*)

Oregon grape (*Mahonia aquifolium*)
Silver lace (*Chrysanthemum ptarmiciflorum*)

FOR BERRIES

Cotoneaster
Heavenly bamboo (*Nandina*), some varieties
Holly

Pyracantha
Silverberry (*Elaeagnus pungens*)

and leaf colors that might accent flowers effectively. Plants with colorful berries are real winter bonuses.

Select cool-season annuals to fill in the arrangement and provide colorful bloom. Also consider winter-blooming bulbs such as amaryllis and paperwhite narcissus. Use cascading plants such as ivy to soften the edges of the arrangement.

PUTTING POTS TOGETHER

Set the largest evergreen foundation plants in place first (if you're using them), position the flowers next (tallest ones first), then add any ground covers and cascading greenery. Place plants close together for a generous, well-filled look. Finally, tuck in cut evergreens and perhaps pine cones and trim with a colorful bow, if you wish.

White ceramic pots hold sophisticated arrangements of winter white and gold. Miniature white cyclamen, gold kalanchoe, and white English primrose provide color and texture; variegated English ivy adds a lively note. Design: Dennis Leong.

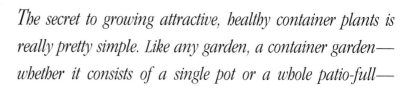

The secret to growing attractive, healthy container plants is really pretty simple. Like any garden, a container garden— whether it consists of a single pot or a whole patio-full—

SECRETS OF
SUCCESS

needs tender, loving care in order to thrive. In the close confines of a container, getting plants off to a good start and providing them with the right care is perhaps even more crucial than it is in the ground.

To ensure success, you'll want to provide the best possible growing environment right from the beginning—suitable pots, good soil, and a location that suits your plants' needs for sun or shade. As it grows, a plant in a pot can't reach into outlying soil for nutrients and moisture. Monitoring water therefore becomes the most important part of container plant care. And because nutrients in the soil are leached out by watering, you'll need to replenish them from time to time. You'll also need to trim, divide, and repot plants from time to time, too, or they'll outgrow their pots.

If this sounds daunting, it needn't be. Basic guidelines for planting and caring for a container garden are presented in simple, down-to-earth steps in the following pages. From planting to watering to protecting plants from the elements, you'll find advice to help you give your plants the best possible start—and keep them going.

Annuals, bulbs, perennials—their success as container plants starts
with proper planting in the right potting mix.

GETTING READY

You've got your pots and your plants, and you're all set to put them together. Here's how to get everything ready for planting in order to get your container garden off to a successful start. It all begins with proper container preparation and the right potting soil for your plants.

HOW MUCH POTTING MIX?

A 2-cubic-foot bag of potting mix is enough to transplant 8 to 10 plants from 1-gallon nursery cans into individual 10- to 12-inch pots. Or the same bag will more than fill a planter box 36 by 8 by 10 inches.

USING SOIL POLYMERS

Superabsorbent polymers are gels that can absorb hundreds of times their weight in water. Mixed into potting soil, they hold onto both water and dissolved nutrients to keep them available near plant roots. Soil polymers let you stretch the time between waterings, and they help to eliminate wide fluctuations of moisture between waterings.

Do you need to use polymers? They're most useful in drier climates, or where dry spells can be expected—or if you're erratic with watering. Containers that tend to dry out quickly—such as hanging baskets—can benefit from soil polymers, too.

You can buy commercial potting mixes with gel already added, or mix it in yourself. It's important to use gels in the manufacturer's recommended proportions; soil that stays too wet can kill your plants.

PREPARING YOUR POTS

Once you've chosen your containers—based on the guidelines in "All about Containers," starting on page 17—make sure they're clean and properly prepared. If you're using a brand-new pot, be sure it has adequate drainage (see page 19), and rinse it out. Submerge terra-cotta pots in clean water (in a large tub or a clean garbage can) to soak thoroughly so they won't draw water away from the soil when you plant.

If you're reusing a container, empty out the old soil and clean the pot well to keep from infesting new plants with any pests and diseases that might be left on the surface. To assure yourself of a pest-free pot, use a stiff brush to scrub the inside with a solution of 1 part bleach and 4 parts hot water. Scrub any stains and dirt from the outside, too, and rinse thoroughly inside and out with clear water.

Cover the drainage hole to keep soil from washing out and pests from crawling in. You can cut a small piece of fine wire screening or use one of the new ready-made screens for containers. The time-honored practice is to put a broken shard, or scrap, of pottery over the hole, edges curving down, but this method does present a greater chance of slowing the flow of water.

You can reuse old soil from containers if it's not compacted and the plants growing in it showed no signs of disease or pests. Break up the soil, pull out old plant roots, and mix in some organic matter and some well-rotted manure or controlled-release fertilizer.

THE RIGHT POTTING SOIL

You might assume that regular garden soil can be used to fill your pots. But garden soil, even good loam, is just too dense to use by itself in containers. Most plants in pots need a lighter soil that's fast-draining and supplies ample nutrients—a special potting mix. In fact, commercial potting mix doesn't even contain soil. Instead, it's a mixture of organic material, mineral matter, limestone, and nutrients.

ORGANIC MATERIAL. This usually consists of peat moss or bark and some form of compost. The organic material should promote good aeration and hold water well. Look for Canadian sphagnum peat moss (not just "peat moss," which may be inferior). Mixes that contain ground-up bark rather than peat moss will probably be less expensive but more likely to compact over time—so be sure they also contain perlite or pumice. The best bark is composted.

The compost in potting mix should be nutrient-rich and lightweight. It may be fir bark, sawdust, mushroom, or something else—but many labels don't list the kind that's used.

MINERAL MATTER. Perlite, vermiculite, pumice, and sand improve drainage. The best mixes contain 10% to 15% perlite or pumice. Sand is cheaper but doesn't hold water and can be heavy; mined sand is best, since it's coarse and doesn't clog air space.

LIMESTONE. This balances the acidity of peat moss. Dolomite limestone is preferable—but it may or may not be identified on the bag.

NUTRIENTS. These are fertilizers, but labels often don't give a breakdown of what's included.

WETTING AGENTS. These help peat moss absorb moisture. Soil polymers (water-absorbing gels) are also sometimes included (see facing page).

POTTING MIX POINTERS

Bag labels often aren't very precise, so finding the best mix for your plants can be a process of trial and error. Choose one made especially for containers. Read the label to be sure all ingredients are listed. For the best success:

- Flush soil with water once or twice before planting to minimize the chances of burning plants with nitrogen or salts.
- Follow the manufacturer's directions for fertilizing.
- Keep unused mix in a sealed container so it doesn't dry out.

MAKING YOUR OWN POTTING MIX

If you're planning an especially large planting or want a special blend, you can doctor a commercial mix or make your own from one of the recipes given at right.

Adjust the amounts according to how much you need. For a small batch, mix in a wheelbarrow or big tub, or on a sheet of plastic. For a larger amount, toss sand and organic material on a big plastic tarp to mix thoroughly, then scatter on fertilizer and limestone. Toss again once or twice to blend.

Store your mix, tightly covered, in a new garbage can or other clean, dry container.

NO-SOIL POTTING MIXES

If you need a large volume of potting mix, you may be able to save money by making your own. The basic mix is made with nitrogen-free fertilizer, so it can be stored up to a year. (Nitrogen dissipates more quickly than the potassium and phosphorus used in this mix.) If you plant during the growing season, use a complete fertilizer about 2 weeks after planting.

BASIC NO-SOIL MIX

You can use this for all but acid-loving plants. These amounts will make nearly 1 cubic yard (9 cubic feet) of mix.

⅔ cubic yard nitrogen-stabilized bark or Canadian sphagnum peat moss
⅓ cubic yard washed 20-grit sand
6 pounds 0-10-10 dry fertilizer
10 pounds dolomite or dolomite limestone

ACID NO-SOIL MIX

Use this mix for azaleas, rhododendrons, camellias, heather, and other acid-loving plants.

4 or 5 parts coarse peat moss
1 part leaf mold

CUSTOMIZING COMMERCIAL MIXES

Here's how to tailor commercially packaged potting mixes for special container needs.

EXTRA-LIGHTWEIGHT MIX

Use this for hanging baskets or other locations where weight is a consideration. It dries out quickly—be sure to monitor watering needs.

2 parts commercial potting mix *or* Basic No-Soil Mix (above)
1 part perlite or vermiculite

RICH MIX

Plants grown for their foliage—like lettuce, caladium, and hosta—may benefit from extra-rich potting soil. Mix timed-release fertilizer into the mix when you plant, according to package directions.

2 parts commercial potting mix
1 part well-composted chicken manure
1 part redwood soil conditioner

PLANTING TIME

Most of your container planting will probably involve moving plants from nursery containers or cell-packs into pots of fairly standard shapes and sizes. You'll use some containers to show off single plants—perhaps under-planted with a low-growing companion. Other pots may be literally stuffed with plants. Here's how to get all of them planted.

BASIC GUIDELINES

Assemble your prepared pots (see page 98), potting mix, and plants. Place extra-large pots where you want them to be positioned permanently—they'll be hard to move once they're planted. Put any necessary saucers or trivets underneath these big containers before you add potting mix.

If you're combining several plants in one container, try arranging them while the plants are still in their nursery pots to see how they look best. Then follow these steps to move your plants into their new containers:

1 Water plants thoroughly in their nursery containers. Moist soil from their nursery pots will cling to the roots—the more the better.

2 Remove plants from their nursery containers as described on the facing page.

3 Check plant roots. Lightly separate matted roots. If a plant is rootbound (its roots tightly twined around the root ball), score the roots lightly with a sharp knife. Gently untangle roots with your fingers.

4 Pour potting mix into the container—enough to hold the top, or crown, of the root ball about 1 inch below the pot rim. (The mix should be moist enough to form a ball when squeezed, but not soaking wet.) If you're combining plants of varying sizes in one container, allow for the one with the deepest root ball first; add soil as you add plants, so that all will be at the same level when you're finished.

5 Position plants in the container, filling in with more moist potting mix around them; press the mix in firmly to plug any air pockets, but don't pack it densely.

6 Water thoroughly. Set small pots in a pan of water and let stand until the soil surface is moist. Gently water larger containers from the top (use a watering can with sprinkler attachment or hose with very fine spray) until water runs out the drainage hole. If water passes through quite rapidly, tamp the soil to firm it; if the water sits on top, loosen the soil carefully with a sharp, thin stick.

If you're using a container without any drainage hole, add water equal to ¼ the soil volume.

POTTING, PLANT BY PLANT

Here's how to remove plants from their nursery containers—or transfer burlap-wrapped and bare-root plants into containers.

CELL-PACKS. Remove plants by carefully pushing on the bottom of individual cells with your thumbs. Tip the plant out, cradling the roots in your palm.

For these small plants, you can fill your container with potting mix to within an inch of the rim, then dig individual plant holes with your fingers or a trowel.

SMALL POTS. Run a knife around the pot's inside edge, then invert the pot and tap it gently to loosen the plant. Let the plant drop out, steadying the root ball with one hand and holding the stem gently between two fingers. Plant as previously outlined in the basic planting steps.

GALLON AND LARGER POTS. If the nursery container is plastic, lay it on its side and gently roll it from side to side to loosen the plant, tap the sides or bottom sharply, or run a knife around the inside edge. If the container is metal and you can't easily remove the plant, use tin snips to cut down the sides. (Be *very* careful—the cut edges are razor-sharp!) In either case, turn the can on its side and gently pull the plant free. Follow the basic planting steps.

PAPER PULP POTS. Remove the plant the same as for gallon-size metal or plastic cans. Or simply punch scattered 2-inch holes into the thick paper sides, then cut or tear off the pot rim to just below the soil level. Place the plant, pot and all, in its new container and fill in around pot sides with potting mix. Eventually the paper pot will decompose into the potting soil.

BARE-ROOT PLANTS. If roots are slightly dried, soak overnight in water before planting to revive them. Then mound soil firmly in the bottom of the container and position the roots over the soil mound, keeping the plant's crown level with the container rim. Finish according to the basic planting steps.

BURLAP-WRAPPED PLANTS. Make sure the material around the plant is natural burlap that will decompose—not plastic. Remove the twine around the top and trim away the upper edge of the burlap, leaving the root ball covered. Then follow the basic planting steps. If the burlap is synthetic, carefully remove it before planting.

Bare-root rose is set on mounded soil with bud union just below level of pot rim, then soil is added to cover the roots.

BULBS—A SPECIAL CASE

For container bulbs, the ideal potting mix includes equal parts of peat moss, other organic material (such as compost or leaf mold), and builder's sand (or perlite for Group 2 bulbs in the chart on page 43). Mix in a complete fertilizer according to label directions. For bulbs that will stay or be replanted in containers longer than a year (Groups 2 and 3), select a pot at least 12 inches deep to allow for root growth.

As a general guide, you should plant bulbs from Group 1 (page 43) with their pointed ends facing up just beneath the soil surface; space close together for a "bouquet" effect, as shown at left, and cover with potting mix. Bulbs from Groups 2 and 3 should be planted a few inches apart, as deep as recommended for individual types (consult your nursery, a bulb catalog, or Sunset's *Bulbs*).

Water newly-planted bulbs well, filling the container to the rim with water and letting it drain 2 or 3 times. Then you need water only enough to keep soil from drying out until new growth appears. Check the pots after about 8 weeks—if leaf tips are poking through the soil or you can see roots in the drainage holes, move the containers to a sunny spot and begin normal watering.

TENDER, LOVING CARE

Regular container maintenance includes the same basic jobs that any garden requires—watering, feeding, and controlling garden pests. But in container gardening, you need to use extra vigilance because of the special limits placed on plants by their containers. And you'll want to keep weeds pulled if they show up in your containers—besides spoiling the picture you're trying to create with your pots, weeds steal nutrients and water from your container plants.

SOIL DRYING OUT?

When the soil in pots is drying out too quickly, try one or more of these solutions.

DOUBLE UP by putting one container inside another; fill the space in between with damp peat moss and cover the soil with small pebbles to conserve moisture further.

REPOT a rootbound plant into a container one size larger.

SWITCH to a container made of less porous material (see page 19).

MULCH the soil surface with pebbles or bark.

GROUP POTS close together so they shelter and shade one another.

TOP PRIORITY: WATERING

Watering is the single most important job in container care. Plants in containers have a limited amount of soil from which to draw moisture, so they tend to require more frequent watering than plants in the ground.

The easiest way to decide if a container plant needs watering is to poke your finger into the top inch of soil; if it feels dry, it's time to water. But keep in mind that different plants have different water requirements. Some need soil that's always moist, while others fare best if soil is allowed to dry out somewhat. Ask about specific plants at the nursery where you purchase them, or consult Sunset's *National Garden Book* or *Western Garden Book*.

As a rule, lightweight soil mixes dry out faster than heavier ones. And plants will probably need extra watering in hot, dry, or windy weather. In *very* hot weather, some (such as hanging baskets) may need watering 2 or 3 times a day.

When you water, give each container enough water to moisten all the soil, not just the top few inches. You'll know the soil is saturated when water runs freely from the drainage hole. When watering a drainless container, add water equal to about ¼ the volume of soil.

A good old watering can is the time-honored way to water container plants; be sure yours has a spout attachment to deliver water in a gentle shower.

When a saucer under a container is full of water, empty it within a day; water allowed to stand much longer will keep the soil soggy. (Use a bulb-type baster to remove water from saucers under big containers.)

WAYS TO WATER

You may enjoy puttering around the garden on your daily rounds, watering each pot by hand as needed. Or you may be always on the go and in need of a dependable automatic system for keeping containers watered. The technique you choose depends on your own personal routine as well as the size and location of your container collection.

No matter how you water, always apply the water in a gentle stream or spray; a strong flow can displace soil and damage plant roots.

WATERING CAN. This may be your choice if you have just a few containers. Use a can with a "rose"—a sprinkler head that screws onto the spout.

GARDEN HOSE. Most container plants can be watered with a gentle trickle of water from a hose onto the soil surface. Attach a flow head that will break the force of the water so that you can deliver water quickly without blasting soil out of your pots. Add a rigid extender tube for long reaches and an on-off valve for convenience. An angled extender tube is useful for hanging plants.

One caution: Water from a hose that's been baking in the sun can be hot enough to damage plants; run it until it's fairly cool before watering.

DRIP IRRIGATION. An irrigation system can make watering effortless. A drip system delivers small amounts of water to individual containers through a network of thin tubes and emitters; you customize the layout according to your particular needs. Water is delivered slowly, soaking each plant's root area with little loss to evaporation or runoff.

The flexible tubing of a drip system can run unobtrusively along a fence, wall, or patio (or even underneath a deck). You can even install an overhead system to send tubes down into hanging containers.

You can connect your drip system to a hose end or directly to the main water source. Either way, you can install an automatic timer if you wish, especially useful for when you're away from home. Drip system kits are available from nurseries, garden centers, hardware stores, and mail-order catalogs.

SUBMERSION. For small containers and hanging baskets, watering by submersion is a real timesaver, especially during hot spells. A good soak can keep soil moist all day and revive plants when soil has become dangerously dry. Simply lower the pot into a tub of water (covering the pot rim but not the plant itself) and keep it there for about a half hour. This technique is also useful for terra-cotta pots from time to time, since they tend to dry out.

GOING ON VACATION?

If you're going away and don't have a plant-sitter, try some of the moisture-conserving suggestions listed on the facing page, or use one of these ideas:

SHELTER POTS under a shade-giving tree.

DIG A TRENCH, fill it with wet sawdust or peat, and set pots in the filler almost up to their rims.

USE WICKS to water pots grouped in a shady spot around a wide, water-filled container. Buy nylon wicks from a nursery or garden center, or cut lengths of thin cotton clothesline. Push one end of a wick 1 to 2 inches into the soil of each pot and put the other end in the water. This can actually keep plants watered for up to a month.

Drip irrigation tubing is the perfect watering solution for plants in hanging baskets, like this lettuce.

DRAINAGE SOLUTIONS

WHEN WATER DOESN'T DRAIN . . . the drainage hole may be blocked. Turn the pot on its side and push a pointed stick or large nail into the hole to unblock it.

WHEN WATER DRAINS TOO FAST. . . there's probably air space between the soil and the container walls. Completely submerge the container in a tub of water for about a half hour. For a large pot, set a hose on the soil surface near the plant's base, adjust the flow to a trickle, and water for up to half an hour, until the soil is saturated.

FEEDING YOUR PLANTS

Plants in the ground can reach out with their roots for nutrients in the soil, but plants in containers depend on you to replenish nutrients.

If you've used a potting mix that contains nutrients, you won't need to fertilize until about 4 to 6 weeks after planting. Follow the guidelines on the potting mix package—or make your own extra-rich soil mix (see page 99). If your soil isn't enriched, you can mix fertilizer in at planting time or begin fertilizing in 1 or 2 weeks if you're planting during the active growing season.

As a general rule, give plants regular doses of fertilizer from spring through summer or autumn, while they're actively growing, and withhold it in late autumn and winter. Follow package directions; once every 2 to 4 weeks should be often enough for most flowers and vegetables.

Containers filled with many plants may need extra fertilizer and more frequent watering to ensure good performance.

FERTILIZER PRIMER

You'll find a bewildering array of fertilizers at the nursery, in various forms and formulas. Here's some of the basic terminology.

COMPLETE FERTILIZERS are any that contain nitrogen (N), phosphorus (P), and potassium (K). The ratio of these ingredients is stated on the label—5-10-10 fertilizer, for example, contains 5% N by weight and 10% each P and K. If any of the three numbers is higher than the others, the fertilizer is considered high in that ingredient.

High-nitrogen fertilizer encourages foliage growth; it's the most important ingredient, but because it's water soluble it's also the most easily depleted. Phosphorus and potassium, the other major nutrients, are virtually insoluble and need to be mixed into the soil at planting time to benefit the entire root system.

SPECIAL-PURPOSE FERTILIZERS are sold for roses, citrus trees, and acid-loving plants like rhododendrons and camellias.

ORGANIC FERTILIZERS have nutrients derived solely from the remains or by-products of once-living organisms, as opposed to manufactured chemical fertilizers. Aged manure, fish emulsion, and bonemeal are examples of organic fertilizers. Usually organic fertilizers are high in just one of the three major nutrient groups—nitrogen, phosphorus, or potassium.

WHAT FORM?

You'll find chemical fertilizers in three basic forms. Of these, many gardeners find liquid or timed-release formulas the easiest to use for containers. With them, there's less chance of burning plants than with dry fertilizer—a greater issue in the confined space of pots than it is in the ground.

LIQUID FERTILIZER (most often crystals or powder that you dissolve in water) is easy to apply, supplies nutrients immediately, and—if you follow label directions—never burns foliage or roots. It's also easily diluted to to suit individual plant needs. Give a half-strength dose once every 2 to 4 weeks during the active growth period.

DRY FERTILIZER is convenient for slow-growing trees and shrubs because it is likely to be a little longer lasting than liquid preparations. Water thoroughly before and after application to avoid any chance of burning roots.

TIMED/CONTROLLED-RELEASE FERTILIZER capsules, either mixed into the potting soil or scattered on the surface and scratched in, diffuse through the soil a little with each watering—great for forgetful or over-busy gardeners. Capsules stay active for varying lengths of time, usually 3 to 8 months (check label).

Fertilizer forms, clockwise from left, include liquid-soluble crystals (mounded and dissolved in water), dry granules, organic fish meal, and timed-release pellets.

A layer of stones helps discourage cats and squirrels from disturbing the soil.

PEST PATROL

The best way to avoid pests and diseases is to maintain healthy growing conditions. If plants are robust and healthy, they'll be more resistant to disease and less likely to attract pests. As preventive medicine, do the following:

- Use clean containers and sterile potting soil mix.

- Keep containers free of weeds, fallen fruit, and dead flowers and leaves.

- Raise containers off the ground to make them less attractive to crawling pests.

- Keep plants well watered and cared for.

If you do discover disease or pests, treat immediately and isolate affected plants for a couple of weeks so problems don't spread. Try the least toxic control measure initially; move on to one of greater toxicity only if the first method is ineffective.

Many gardeners today opt for natural and mechanical controls for pests instead of chemical insecticides. These include hosing off small insects such as aphids, washing plants with nontoxic soaps, hand-picking pests such as slugs and snails (deposit in soapy water to kill them), and introducing biological controls such as ladybird beetles that eat plant-destroying insects.

Consider using naturally derived sprays such as insecticidal soaps, botanical insecticides, and horticultural oils. You can make your own soap spray by mixing a teaspoon of dishwashing liquid and a teaspoon of cooking oil into a spray bottle of water (about ½-quart size). Spray on affected parts of plants as needed when aphids, whiteflies, or other small insects attack. Do this in the morning so that plants have a chance to dry off during the day.

For more information about dealing with specific pests and plant diseases, consult Sunset's *Western Garden Problem Solver* or *Garden Pests and Diseases* book or *Garden Problem Solver* CD-ROM, or check with your nursery or county agricultural extension service.

MOVING HEAVY POTS

One big advantage of plants in containers is that they can take center stage when they're looking and "acting" their best, then be moved off to the wings. But a rhododendron in an 18-inch box can tip the scales at 200 pounds. Clearly, you'll need a crew of stagehands or some simple mechanical help to move that bloomer.

Of course, it's best to put big containers in their permanent locations when you plant them, or set them on lockable wheels to start with. But when that's not possible, try one of the following techniques.

For the safest and easiest move, enlist a helper. Attaching handles to container sides or cleats to the bottom makes it easier to get a grip. And move containers before watering—you don't need the extra weight of wet soil.

SLIDE a big container along a level surface on a big piece of heavy cardboard; roll or fold over an edge to give yourself a good grip. Or use a sturdy burlap bag or old throw rug.

You can also slip a wide-bladed shovel under a container to slide it over grass, dirt, exposed aggregate concrete, or gravel. Avoid brick, tile, wood, or other surfaces that might scratch.

ROLL a round container—just tip it on edge and rotate it, with a helper to steady it.

LET WHEELS move your container—lift it onto a dolly that you've purchased or made with three or four 2-inch industrial casters mounted on a piece of 1-inch plywood. Casters might also be permanently attached to a container. (Be sure wheels are lockable; a runaway container is a potential disaster!)

A strong metal hand truck is a good investment if you move heavy containers frequently; for safety, tie on the container with rope. You can also purchase wagons made especially for hauling plants.

MAKE ROLLERS by using three or four dowels or lengths of pipe to move broad-bottomed tubs along smooth, level surfaces. As you roll the container along, pick up the rollers from behind and place them in front. To round a corner, fan out the rollers.

MAKE A RAMP from a sheet of heavy-duty plywood to pull a container up a short flight of steps. Tie a strong rope around the container (this works best for containers with rims) and have a helper steady the base of the ramp.

WEATHERIZING YOUR PLANTS

Plants in containers are even more vulnerable to extremes of weather than their in-ground counterparts. You'll want to choose plants and containers that suit your particular conditions to begin with. But even in the mildest of climates, nature can provide some challenges. You'll need a few tricks up your sleeve to protect your plants when hot spells, wind, drought, frost, and freezes conspire to get the best of them.

HEAT AND WIND

No container plant will thrive in constant drying winds or unrelieved heat, no matter how much you water it. Avoid putting containers against bare fences, stark walls, or other structures that reflect intense heat from the sun. If you live in a windy location, you may want to screen container plants from the wind—even by planting in-ground plants to act as a windbreak, if that's possible.

When conditions are temporarily hot or otherwise extreme, it's best to move containers under an overhang, shade tree, or patio umbrella. Be particularly careful to give them enough water.

IF PLANTS FREEZE. . .

If you wake in the morning to find that your plants have been subjected to freezing weather, you can try to save them by shifting them right away to a lighted garage or basement that's cold but not freezing. Let plants thaw slowly, without trying to speed up the process; then move them to a protected spot outdoors. Don't prune frost-damaged stems until just before new growth begins.

DRY AS BONES

Another enemy of container gardening is drought—not just prolonged absence of rain, but any ongoing drying conditions. If you live in a dry-climate area, place your containers in the spots within your garden or patio where they'll get cooling shade at midday. And consider these water-saving strategies:

- Plant in the largest possible containers; the larger the pot, the more slowly the soil will dry out.
- Paint the interior walls of porous pots (wood, clay) with sealant for greater moisture retention (see page 23).
- Add water-holding soil polymers to the soil (see page 98).
- Mulch the soil surface with a 1- to 2-inch layer of bark, rough compost, gravel, or cobblestones.
- Double-pot smaller containers; add gravel, peat moss, or soil between the two pots.
- Group pots; they'll help shade one another.
- Install a drip irrigation system on a timer, so that plants get regular but not excessive doses of water (see page 103).
- Select unthirsty plants. Consider succulents, herbs, annuals such as sweet alyssum, perennials such as erigeron, and some ornamental grasses. Look for attractive native plants or others that came from similar climates elsewhere.

ABOVE: To insulate a large pot in cold weather, tie on a jacket of plastic bubble wrap.

BELOW: Double-potting is one of the best ways to conserve moisture in the soil; here, a plastic outer pot and a layer of gravel keep soil in inner terra-cotta pot from drying out.

WHEN FROST THREATENS

In areas where frost is sometimes a danger, extra effort is required to maintain container plants through the winter. Shift pots to a protected place at the first hint of dipping temperatures. Place them under a tree, a porch overhang, or eaves; the idea is to protect plants from exposure to the open sky. If containers are too heavy to move, you can try one of the following:

COVER THE PLANT. Use a sheet of heavy plastic, a garbage bag, burlap, or an old sheet, held up with stakes to keep it from touching foliage. A cardboard box works to cover smaller plants. Cut out the bottom and slip the box over the plant; open the top flaps during the day to let in the sunlight, then close at night.

INSULATE THE CONTAINER. Wrap it with burlap sacks or plastic bubble wrap, tied on with string.

MULCH POTS. Add a layer of peat moss, wood chips, or straw over the soil in containers.

GROUP CONTAINERS. Position pots close together and they'll provide some mutual protection.

DEEP FREEZE

In extreme-cold areas where winter brings hard freezes, an outdoor container garden is definitely a spring-to-fall pleasure only. No matter how hardy the plant, its roots won't survive constant freezing temperatures in an above-ground container.

In such a climate, if you want to plant something besides annuals in pots, you'll have to plan on moving them indoors or— if they're hardy for your climate zone—removing them from their containers in the fall and planting them out in the garden.

MOVING INDOORS. If you're going to move containers indoors, you need to provide them with lots of light. Tropical plants especially will need a west or south window, since their growing season is year-round. Other plants may go dormant. And, of course, you'll need a good amount of space in which to house container plants. Dormant plants can stay in a well-lighted garage or basement that doesn't freeze, or in an unheated room of the house.

Plants that keep their leaves in winter shouldn't be moved abruptly into a warm area; give them a few days in a transitional zone, such as a protected porch. (Deciduous plants that go dormant in winter will be less sensitive.) The months spent indoors will be stressful for plants; withhold fertilizer and carefully monitor watering through the winter.

One way to simplify the chore of moving plants in winter is to double-pot them. Plant them in lightweight, easy-to-move plastic pots which you can set inside larger decorative containers. The inner and outer containers can be moved separately when fall chills come.

STAYING OUTDOORS. Some hardy deciduous trees and shrubs, such as Japanese maples and hydrangeas, can be overwintered in their containers using something akin to the "Minnesota tip" method of overwintering rose bushes. Once the plant has dropped all its leaves, you dig a 10- to 12-inch-deep trench in which you tip the plant in its container over on its side. Then cover container and plant with leaves and plastic sheeting for insulation.

POT PROTECTION. Containers themselves suffer from freezing and thawing cycles, too. Clay pots fare poorly, because any moisture they absorb will freeze and cause them to crack. Even plastic pots tend to become very brittle and crack when frozen. Wood containers will survive but will take a beating. Fiberglass or heavy stone or concrete containers are less likely to be damaged by freezing; these can be emptied and left outside to overwinter, if necessary.

If you have big clay pots that you simply can't move indoors, try this: after digging up the plants, sink a 2-inch-wide shaft of plastic foam (from a home supply or craft store) down the center of the pot through the soil. When moisture in the soil freezes and expands, the foam will be compressed, taking pressure off the container walls.

GOOD GROOMING

Like in-ground plants, container plants perform and look their best when you're conscientious about pruning to shape and neaten them, encourage fullness, and reduce size when needed. In fact, since container plants may be viewed at closer range than in-ground plants, keeping them tidy takes on added importance.

DEADHEADING

Most annual and perennial flowering plants benefit from having their spent blossoms cut or pinched off during the growing season. Deadheading, as this is called, keeps the plant from using its energy to set seed; the result is a longer blooming period—and a more attractive plant.

PINCHING

Pinching off growth tips encourages a bushier, more compact plant shape and more blossoms. You can do this when plants are still quite young—in fact, many annuals benefit from being pinched back as soon as you plant them.

Using your thumb and finger, just nip off the tender growing tip (the terminal bud) of a branch or stem; the plant will respond by putting out side shoots instead. Pinch the plant wherever you want it to branch outward. For the densest foliage, start pinching while stems are short; this gives you branching closer to the plant's center, resulting in a denser plant. Keep pinching as needed throughout the growing season, but not so much that you remove flower buds you want to bloom.

Make pruning cuts just above a part of the plant that will continue to grow.

Flowering plants look and bloom best when you regularly remove spent blossoms—and don't forget to pick a few fresh ones for a bouquet!

OTHER PRUNING

To keep shrubs looking attractive, and proportional to their containers, you'll need to shape and thin them from time to time. Some plants (such as roses) can benefit from annual pruning, with occasional clipping during the growing season. Other shrubs, some vines, and a few trees may need periodic thinning of weak, superfluous, or dead branches. Clip off wayward growth regularly so you won't have to prune it later on.

Basic pruning cuts should be made about ¼ inch above some part that will continue to grow: a growth bud (at the base of a leaf or on a leafless stem), another branch, or the trunk. Don't leave stubs, as these invite disease. And be sure to use sharp tools, so cuts will seal over cleanly.

THINNING is pruning to eliminate entire stems and branches. Roses, fruit trees, and berry bushes—and many other shrubs, trees, and vines—perform best if thinned from time to time to open up the branch structure and clear out unproductive limbs.

HEADING is pruning to remove only part of a stem or branch by cutting it back to a growth bud or twig. Do this to force branching below the cut.

SHEARING—actually a form of heading—helps keep plants with dense foliage, such as boxwood and juniper, neatly shaped. Use hedge shears or hand clippers to shear as often as necessary throughout the growing season to create a uniform shape and an even surface.

AT SEASON'S END

Perennials and bulbs both need a bit of attention at the end of their bloom periods to keep them going for successive years.

PERENNIALS

When their last flowers fade in summer or autumn, shrubby or branching perennials (such as chrysanthemums and yarrow) need to be cut back to encourage the best bloom the following season. Use pruning shears to remove about one-third to one-half the length of each stem. Don't cut back clump-forming perennials (such as primroses and gerbera).

BULBS

After they finish blooming, your container bulbs—and tubers, corms, and rhizomes—need a special kind of care. Refer to the groupings on page 43 to decide which of the following treatments your bulbs need.

GROUP 1 BULBS, like tulips and crocus, should be planted out in the garden after one bloom season—they don't do well in containers for more than a season. Dig them out of their pots after foliage yellows and store them until it's time to plant again, as described below.

GROUP 2 BULBS, such as tuberous begonias and dahlias, need to be dug up and stored out of soil, then repotted in fresh soil in late winter/early spring for another season. Take them out of their containers when foliage has yellowed, and store as described below.

OFF-SEASON STORAGE

To store bulbs, remove leaves and soil and then spread the bulbs on newspapers in a shaded spot to dry for a week or two. It's best not to separate bulbs before you store them—broken surfaces can let in disease organisms.

Bulbs that have a hard protective skin or a covering that peels off, such as daffodils, can be hung in mesh bags or piled loosely in boxes or baskets. Bulbs that lack such protective coverings, such as tuberous begonias and dahlias, should be placed in a single layer in cardboard or wooden boxes or clay pots and covered with sand, vermiculite, sawdust, perlite, ground bark, or peat moss.

Store in a cool, dry place. At planting time, you can divide and replant them in containers (for Group 2 bulbs) or in the ground.

GROUP 3 BULBS, such as amaryllis and lily, can stay in the same container and soil for several seasons. Move them to a sheltered place (or indoors) before the first frost. Stop watering deciduous bulbs when leaves yellow, until new shoots poke up or it's normal planting time for the next growing season, whichever happens first. Move them to good light when growth appears.

Evergreen bulbs in this group—such as clivia—will need water even when they're not actively growing; keep the container in a cool, lighted room and water sparingly until the growing season begins. (In mild climates, they can stay outdoors all winter.)

Different bulbs need to be stored differently in winter. Store bulbs with hard skins so that air can circulate around them, as in hanging mesh bags (TOP). Bulbs that lack protective skin need covered storage (BOTTOM). Keep both kinds in a cool, dry place until planting time.

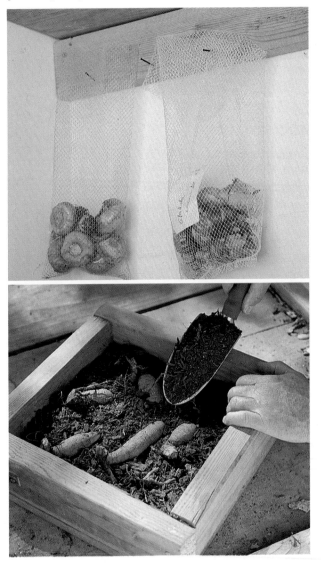

TUNE-UPS FOR PERENNIALS, SHRUBS, AND TREES

Sooner or later, most perennials, shrubs, and trees begin to crowd their pots. Then they may need a tune-up in order to go back into the same pot, or they may need to be shifted to a bigger pot. Even plants that benefit from being somewhat potbound will eventually need repotting.

Most container perennials do fine with basic clipping, watering, and feeding for the first couple of years but begin to look straggly and crowded by around the third year. Shrubs and small trees usually need attention every three years or so, depending on their growth rate.

How do you know when a plant is outgrowing its pot? If roots are matted or poking through the drainage hole, or if plants just look stressed-out, it's time to repot. You'll probably need to divide a plant you're repotting or trim its roots—a job best done in the fall, when active growth slows, or in early spring if you live in a cold-winter area.

MINOR TUNE-UP

If container perennials are less than two years old, or if you divided them the previous year, they'll only need a light tune-up to perk them up. Cut branching-type plants back at the end of the growing season as described on page 109. Then use a screw-driver to poke three 1-inch holes about 6 to 8 inches deep in the soil (keep holes about 2 inches away from plant crowns to avoid damaging roots). Drop about a teaspoon of complete fertilizer into each hole and cover with soil. Lightly scratch the soil surface and add about an inch of compost or topsoil.

MAJOR TUNE-UP

After a plant has been in a container for about three years, or is looking less healthy, here's how to refresh it by trimming or dividing its roots and replanting it back into the same pot:

REMOVE PLANTS FROM THE POT. Loosen the soil around the pot walls with a knife. If you're dealing with a large tub, let the soil dry slightly, then lay the tub on its side (protect chippable pots with cloth). Tap around the rim with a rubber mallet and pull the plant free. Or float the root ball out by forcing water from a hose through the drainage hole. Remove the plant gently; be careful not to injure bark.

EXAMINE THE ROOT BALL. If plant roots are twisted and wound around the root ball, they need to be trimmed. To prune the roots of shrubs or trees, first pull out and untangle large roots (soil will fall away from the root ball as you do this), then use shears or a pruning saw to cut the big roots back by a third to a half.

DIVIDE PERENNIALS that need it—they may just look crowded, or they may have clumping root systems that spread outward (like daylilies). Using a sharp shovel or knife, make clean cuts through the root ball between plants. For plants that form thick clumps, like lamb's ears and yarrow, you may need to slice through the crown of the plant to make divisions. Keep vigorous outer growth; discard woody or weak portions or any pieces that are shriveled or diseased. Rub some of the old soil off the root ball to make space for fresh soil.

SCRUB THE INSIDE OF THE POT. Use a stiff brush and either plain hot water or a dilute solution of household bleach (4 parts water to 1 part bleach); rinse with clear water. Replace the drainage hole cover.

ADD FRESH POTTING MIX to the clean container. (If plants are disease-free, you can combine fresh potting mix and some composted organic material with part of the old soil, well broken up.)

PLACE THE PLANT (or plant division) back in the pot and add soil to cover the roots, the same as for a new plant (see page 100).

Untangle overgrown roots of trees, then prune back with sharp shears. Expect a shorter container life span for a tree than for many other plants; you can keep going up in pot size, but at some point a tree will do better in the ground.

MOVING UP TO A BIGGER POT

If plant roots are crowded, even after being trimmed, or if the plant just looks too big for its container, it's time to move up to a larger pot. Don't jump many sizes up—plants sitting in too much damp soil run the risk of root rot, especially in wet, cold climates. It's safest to shift to a pot just one size up; fast-growing plants can move up two sizes. Follow the basic planting directions on page 100 to repot a plant.

FRESH START FOR PERENNIALS

1 Cut back plants using hand pruners—to 6 to 12 inches for tall, semishrubby plants like salvia, 2 to 4 inches for mounding and trailing types like lavender or Mexican daisy. (Don't cut back clumping plants, such as lamb's ears.)

2 Carefully remove plants from pot. Use a shovel if roots are dense and hard; rock it back and forth between plants and around the inside of pot.

3 If plants need dividing, like this clump of lamb's ears, cut through crown and root ball with a sharp knife.

4 Repot plants in their container with fresh potting mix.

INDEX

Boldface page numbers *refer to photos. In general, plant names are indexed only when the plant is featured in a photo. To find page references for listings of plants, look under plant categories—annuals, shrubs, vegetables, and so on.*